ART
FROM FOUND
MATERIALS
discarded and natural

Also by Mary Lou Stribling
MOSAIC TECHNIQUES

REVERSE APPLIQUE "mola" from the San Blas Islands, Panama. Scraps of cotton fabrics, layered and pierced to expose underlying patterns and colors. (*Collection of the author.*)

SUMMER FLOWERS. By Mary Lou Stribling. Beach pebbles and colored gravel. Reprinted from *Family Circle* magazine. (*Photograph by George K. Nordhausen. © The Family Circle, Inc., 1969.*)

ENAMELED FLOWERS made from tin can lids. By Mary Lou Stribling.

ART
FROM FOUND
MATERIALS
discarded and natural

by MARY LOU STRIBLING

Crown Publishers, Inc.   New York

To Jim and Katimae

Designed by Shari de Miskey

Contents

Acknowledgments

Credit for the production of this book is owed to many persons, including my husband, family, and friends, who contributed encouragement, advice, and understanding of the priority it had on my time. I appreciate, also, the work of Rich Rains, who printed my negatives, and Susan Croke, who helped with typing.

Thanks to the museums, galleries, and organizations which provided some of my illustrations and helped locate artists whose work was appropriate for my subject. They include: The Bernice P. Bishop Museum, Honolulu; The Brooklyn Museum, New York; The M. H. De Young Memorial Museum, San Francisco; The Museum of Modern Art, New York; The Pasadena (California) Art Museum; Adele Bednarz Galleries, Los Angeles; Anima Mundi Gallery, Mill Valley, Calif.; Bertha Schaefer Gallery, New York; Contemporary Gallery, Dallas; Henry Gallery, Seattle; Little Gallery, Union, N.J.; The Marion Koogler McNay Art Institute, San Antonio; The New York Hilton Hotel; The Saint Paul (Minn.) Art Center; Sankey Gallery, Mendocino, Calif.; The Smithsonian Institution, Washington, D.C.; Southern Highland Handicraft Guild, Asheville, N.C.; the Storm Center, Sausalito, Calif.; Wichita (Kansas) Art Association; Yah-A-Teh Craft Shop, Sausalito, Calif.

Thanks to *Better Homes and Gardens, Ceramics Monthly, Christmas Ideas, Family Circle,* and *Popular Ceramics* for permission to include some of my material which originally appeared in their publications.

I am especially grateful to all the artists represented here who shared so freely their philosophical concepts and working techniques. My own personal horizons have been greatly expanded by our communications.

M. L. S.

List of Color Illustrations

Contributing Artists

FELICIANO BEJAR
ROBERT BIANCALANA
BILL BREWER
LUCILE BROKAW
L. STANLEY CARPENTER
JACKIE CURRY
MARY CASE DEKKER
MAY DESCHAMP
LAURA DEVENDORF
DOMINIC DIMARE
HARRY DIX
DAVID ECKELS
HOWARD GLICK
JOAN GOLDSTEIN
BOB GRAHAM
ART GRANT
ANN GRIFFITH
RONALD GRIFFITHS
JUAN GRIS

EVELYN GULICK
BRIAN HALE
WILMA HARRIS
SYDNEY HERSCHLEB
ANN HUNT
MABEL HUTCHISON
TERRY ILLES
MAGGIE JAGLA
MARIE KELLY
KAY KINNEY
LU LUNDSTROM
MAUDE LYNNE
ROBERT MCCHESNEY
NICK NICKOLDS
ALFONSO OSSORIO
FLORENCE PACKARD
H. G. PASHIGIAN
CHARLOTTE PATERA
LINO PERA

PABLO PICASSO
WILSON PRICE
HENRY RASMUSEN
BILL REILY
HELEN STEINAU RICH
PRISCILLA SAGE
DOROTHY SAUNDERS
ARTHUR SECUNDA
JOAN SESTAK
WENDY SESTAK
ALICE SHANNON
J. RICHARD SORBY
BOB STORM
MARY LOU STRIBLING
MARY TOTTEN
JEAN VARDA
PABLITA VELARDE
SALLY WETHERBY
MARCUS WHITE

(All photographs, art works, and diagrams not otherwise
credited are by the author.)

ix

Foreword

The Found Artist occupies a unique spot in the world of art for he is both a *collector* of things and a *creator* of things. His most prized acquisitions often have little or no commercial worth, but then price tags serve only to establish the desirability of objects in terms of exchange, and may be completely unrelated to how the objects themselves are valued by an individual.

The craftsman's delight in finding treasures in unexpected places is compounded by the satisfaction of "refinding" them in his mind and imagination. With the discovery of art in something disconnected with art, his accumulations no longer retain their old identities since they are no longer associated with the purposes for which they were originally designed. They are changed from finished products with familiar labels to raw materials for the construction of new forms which may have no labels at all. The meanings of these new shapes and compositions are seldom literal, and in many cases will be translated by an observer into something entirely opposed to the intent of the artist. This is one of the most provocative aspects of Found Art, and a reason why it has tremendous appeal for individuals who have the courage to reject popular standards of beauty in a search for values of greater personal significance.

In some ways the medium is extremely demanding. It requires an emotional involvement beyond that of simply making a statement with clay or paints, for we must first make aesthetic judgment of the materials themselves without the security of a manufacturer's recommendation. Next, we must isolate and tenaciously hold to the inspirational elements of these materials, or they may become hopelessly lost in the fascinating process of resurrection.

There are no recipes to guarantee success of

your efforts, but there are technical guides which will greatly facilitate production. You will find such guides in the pages of this book and will discover countless others as your work progresses.

A broad range of subjects has been included to illustrate useful techniques and the many different ways they have been used by craftsmen of today and earlier times. The finished works are remarkably varied and demonstrate the adaptibility of found materials to the interests of decorators, teachers, and amateurs, as well as professional artists.

Formal art training is not a prerequisite for understanding the instruction which follows; however, some familiarity with elementary principles of good design is desirable. Supplementary study material is noted in the Appendix.

There are other needs which cannot actually be supplied by education, though certainly education can point out ways they may be developed. The first of these is perception—awareness and respect for every separate part of the vast world around us, from mountains and oceans to the tiny shells, bones, and manmade debris which line their rims. The second is the creative energy to respond emotionally and physically to what our senses perceive and to the impulses they set in motion.

Most importantly, perhaps, we need a special kind of humility which is related to tolerance for the eccentricities of our fellow man, and recognition of our own fallibilities. It can probably most accurately be described as a sense of humor.

Archeologists have found the history of man in his trash heaps, and Found Artists of today are rewriting the story from the same source. The plot is far less somber—and the task is a great deal more fun!

M. L. S.

Fig. 1. Carved mask from New Ireland, Melanesia. (Photo courtesy of the M. H. De Young Memorial Museum.)

chapter 1

Art: Found and Refound

Many pages in the history of man are blank and perhaps always will be. We do not know exactly what our first ancestors were like, nor the precise moment when they first appeared on this planet. We do know that as far back as thirty to forty thousand years ago their physical and aesthetic capabilities had reached a stage of development that enabled them to produce art.

It is unreasonable to assume, however, that the urge for artistic expression appeared suddenly and dramatically at this specific period of the Old Stone Age. Cro-Magnon Man's title of "First Artist" is purely honorary, and is a result of certain factors of chance which contributed to the survival of his handiwork. One factor was the preserving qualities of the cool, dry air in the caves where his murals were painted. Another was the indestructible nature of the paints he made from oils and colored clays. No doubt, even earlier men had decorated their bodies with natural stains and pigments, or had made drawings on stones or cliffs which were exposed to weather, or had assembled grasses, feathers, seeds, bark, hides, and other perishable materials into decorative arrangements which were too fragile to last more than a short span of time.

It may seem a bit futile to search for beginnings of art before there is universal agreement on what *is* art, but the wide variance in opinions of historians indicates that the word itself, like truth, freedom, beauty, and love, can never be defined in a way that is meaningful to all individuals.

Franz Boas distinguishes man's artistic activities from his struggle for survival by defining them as: ". . . work which gives to them aesthetic pleasure." [1] Whether or not these efforts actually produce art is perhaps another matter, though many historians believe that the intention or attempt to produce art justifies the classification of the product as such. If we

[1] Franz Boas, *Primitive Art* (New York, Dover Publications, Inc., 1955), page 9.

accept this, there still remains the dilemma of establishing guidelines to determine which works are good and which are not.

We can use our own personal preferences as a yardstick ("I don't know anything about art, but I know what I like!"), or accept the standards fixed by society, or those of persons society designates as "authorities." In any case, the evaluations are human and, being so, are influenced by taste, education, prejudice, intellect, and all other facets of our humanness. Further, if we remain open minded, our judgments will stay in a continuing state of flux. Even professional art critics find themselves constantly forced to reverse opinions that become obsolete as our culture grows and changes.

For these reasons, we shall be primarily concerned in the following pages with ways of *accomplishing* the aesthetic activity. And since we cannot separate present accomplishments from earlier activities which have made them possible, we shall take a few backward glances as we go along. We will discover that few processes or materials are really new, but they have been so refined, expanded, disassembled, and recombined by inventive craftsmen that they result in works which are unique to our times.

FOUND ART WAS

Found Art is a term coined to describe works which are composed in part or entirety of natural or salvaged objects. It follows that all primitive craftsmen were Found Artists since they had no other sources for supplies. Art has always played an important role in religious beliefs and rituals, and it is likely that much of the artists' work derived from an attempt to create a kind of sorcery to insure their conquest of food and enemies or to solicit favors from the superior forces they dimly perceived behind the order of nature. As E. O. Christensen puts it: "What man cannot overcome through his own strength, he may attempt to appease and befriend." [2]

[2] E. O. Christensen, *Primitive Art* (New York, Bonanza Books, n.d.), page 67.

But "art for art's sake" is not necessarily an indulgence of modern man, for the love of ornamentation is universal. Although primitive man might have assigned magical qualities to his symbols and images, he undoubtedly also found them beautiful and delighted in the task of their creation.

His earliest efforts were probably simply refinements or embellishments of natural forms which suggested some subject to him, and he was content to bring his own inner vision more clearly into focus with a few gouges or scratches. As he became more advanced, he learned to develop completely original designs through extensive alterations of the found object and often combined several different kinds of materials with it.

These aesthetic activities involved first of all *discovery*. They involved *rediscovery* when the artist physically assigned to the original matter the new identity which had been conceived in his imagination.

Our appreciation of the art works of primitive cultures is not nearly as new as many persons may suppose. It has paralleled our interest in the total structures of these societies, an interest which has become increasingly active since the establishment of ethnological museums in the nineteenth century.

In the beginning, primitive artifacts were simply objects of curiosity because they were related to bizarre and barbarous customs. Ethnologists, as well as the average museum visitor, had little or no regard for their aesthetic merit. Gradually, as museums for ethnic studies were established in larger numbers throughout the civilized world, primitive art forms began to lose some of their strangeness to the lay public, and artists began to discover in them a fresh, new vitality.

It is oversimplification, perhaps, to say that familiarity with and continuing exposure to any new concept foretells its eventual acceptance, for certainly a number of other elements must be simultaneously present. Yet there is little doubt that our discovery of artistic value in the crafts of primitive societies has greatly contributed to our acceptance of the validity of many contemporary expressions which only a few decades ago would have been dismissed as crude or ridiculous.

A study of primitive art clearly reveals that man's emotional need for activities which give him aesthetic pleasure is one of the qualities which distinguishes him from the lower forms of life. Civilization neither created the need nor his capacity to respond to it in one way or another. It has merely provided him with a greater choice of media and has influenced his preferences for the form his expression assumes.

Or has it?

Fig. 2. Mask of Naha Tesho, Zuni Indians, New Mexico. Painted hide, trimmed with horsehair and fibers. (Photo courtesy of the Brooklyn Museum.)

4

Fig. 3. Mask of Kjaklo, Zuni Indians, New Mexico. Painted hide, trimmed with fur, feathers, and yarn. (Photo courtesy of the Brooklyn Museum.)

Fig. 4. Shrine of Kolowisi, Zuni Indians, New Mexico. (Photo courtesy of the Brooklyn Museum.)

Fig. 5. Coiled basket, Yokut Indians, Tulare County, California. (Photo courtesy of the M. H. De Young Memorial Museum.)

FOUND ART IS

Man progressed at different rates in different parts of the world, and time alone did not insure his advancement from primitive to civilized. In fact, there are primitive communities in existence today which have remained basically unchanged for countless generations.

Our appreciation for primitive arts of both the past and present is but one part of our increasing curiosity about and admiration for archaic art, folk crafts, and the art of children and the emotionally disturbed. There is nothing really revolutionary about our interest. We have simply discovered in these works values which are more closely related to our own time than are those of classical Greece and the Old Masters.

This is not to say that we would disallow Phidias and Rembrandt their hallowed places in the annals of art history, but rather that we no longer accept the validity of slavishly imitating their styles of expression. It would be equally invalid to emulate the art of primitive people purely for the sake of producing something "different."

The word *primitive* when applied to art should not be confused with its application to things which are crude, rough, and unpolished. It is generally used to classify art which has been produced by people who have not developed a written language and has nothing to do with excellence or the period in time when it was created.

Primitivism is an entirely different matter,

and it is here that we can find the elusive relationship of contemporary Found Art with that produced by unlettered craftsmen. It lies in basic concepts or philosophies and not necessarily in physical similarities. Primitivism means being concerned with attitude rather than form. It means being concerned with fundamentals instead of superficialities, with emotion rather than technical virtuosity.

Robert Goldwater expresses it this way: ". . . It is the assumption that the further one goes back—historically, psychologically, or aesthetically—the simpler things become; and that because they are simpler they are more profound, more important, and more valuable." [3]

He adds further that the nature of this simplicity varies with the nature of the seekers, and certainly a glance through the examples of works in this book will reveal an astonishing range of forms and compositions, some of which are physically quite complex. But there is, I believe, a common bond. It is partly the primitivist's desire to express something which is *felt,* not merely *seen,* and it is partly his childlike delight in discovering worth in the humble things of the world around him.

Sheldon Cheney calls the distinguishing quality of early inventive design "the spirit of the childhood of art." [4] Childhood in this sense

[3] Robert Goldwater, *Primitivism in Modern Art* (rev. ed., New York, Vintage Books, 1967), page 251.

[4] Sheldon Cheney, *A World History of Art* (New York, The Viking Press, 1939), page 5.

was not intended to designate a phase of growth, but to describe a joyful and inspired youthfulness of expression. This spirit is evident in most of the examples presented here, regardless of whether the artist intended to be profound, playful, satirical, or to merely create some bright accessory to decorate his home or person.

The influence of primitivism in an artist's work is not always clearly evident, nor can it always be isolated. We can, however, see certain elements in the later works of Picasso which reflect his admiration for African sculpture and the paintings of Henri Rousseau. Gauguin's paintings distinctly show his love for the art of Polynesia and Egypt. The works of Miró and Klee demonstrate their interests in the drawings of children and the insane. Each of these artists discovered some facet of primitivism which "spoke" to him, and it served as an inspirational catalyst in his search for a new medium of expression.

Picasso is generally acknowledged as being the first major artist to use found objects in his paintings. About the same time, however, a number of other artists who were active in the Cubist movement began to make similar experiments. The collages of Braque and Gris,

Fig. 6. "Construction with Glove (By the Sea)" by Pablo Picasso. Cardboard, plaster, and wood on canvas, covered with sand. (Photo courtesy of the Museum of Modern Art.)

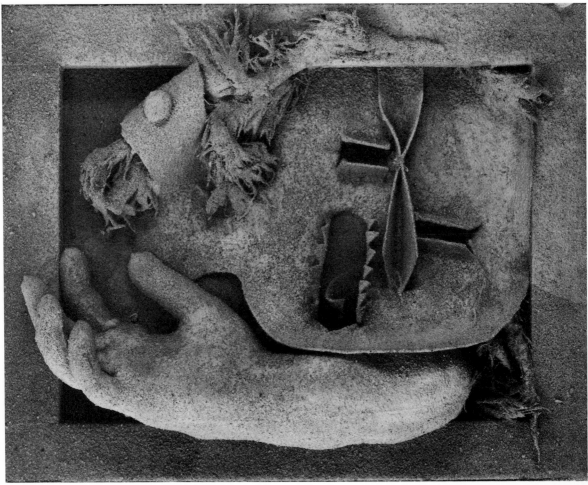

which were made of printed letters, newspapers, wallpaper scraps, bottle labels, corrugated cardboard, and other bits of trivia are especially notable. Braque's affinity with primitivism is revealed in his statement, "I am concerned with attuning myself with nature far more than with copying it." [5]

The Dadaists seized upon Found Art as a means of protest. In their revolt against superficiality and ostentation, they sought to drag art from its sacred pedestal and reduce it to a level of absurdity. It was a cult of meaninglessness and nihilistic satire, and its influence is still active among the Pop Artists of today.

We can see then, that Found Art did not disappear from the earth along with ancient man to suddenly be "refound" in this decade

[5] Jean Cassou, *Braque* (New York, Harry N. Abrams, Inc., n.d.).

of the twentieth century. It has existed all along in one form or another, particularly among the folk craftsmen who continue to produce some of our purest examples.

Novelty may account for a small part of our renewed enthusiasm, for we are a restless, changing society and accept "differentness" more readily than did the previous generation. Novelty may also account for some of the opposition of the traditionalists, since the sensibilities of a large segment of our population are outraged by anything they do not fully comprehend.

It was Picasso, I believe, who said that one should no more try to understand art than to try to understand the song of a bird. I do not claim to understand the songs of all of the works included in this volume, but I have had a great deal of pleasure from listening to their music.

Fig. 7. "Fetish Figure," by Art Grant, is composed of a variety of salvaged objects, including a signal light from a toy train set, a piece of bathroom plumbing, and junk jewelry.

Fig. 8. The body of "Up Tight," by Lino Pera, is an old nutcracker. The position of the head can be changed by turning the screws at the top of the cracker.

Fig. 9. "Knob Ladies" by Lino Pera. Brass doorknobs, cabinet pulls, and assorted hardware.

Fig. 10. Sculpture by Marcus White. Steel pipe cut up and reassembled by welding. (Photo courtesy of the artist.)

Fig. 11. "Music Machine," by Arthur Secunda, looks the way a calliope sounds. The incredible construction has an aerial at the top and includes trembling springs, gears, hair curlers, coat hooks, pin flower holders, junk jewelry, butterflies, and parts of toy instruments. It houses an old fashioned music box. (Photo courtesy of California Design, Pasadena Art Museum.)

Fig. 12. "Fragment" by Marie Kelly. A stitchery hanging of cotton threads, wool yarn, and strings, on a salvaged peanut bag. The design was established by pulling out some of the threads of the foundation and combining them with the other materials into textured masses. Glass marbles were suspended in webs of thread in some of the openings to add the extra dimension of colored light. (Cast silver chalice by William Haendel is a part of the permanent collection of the Saint Paul Art Center. Photo courtesy of the Saint Paul Art Center.)

chapter 2

Thread, Fibers, and Feathers

Man first attempted to meet his need for clothing by draping himself with large leaves or the skins of animals he killed for food, but as early as the New Stone Age he had learned to make garments from coarse fabrics woven from plant fibers.

Linen of an exceptionally fine quality was produced in ancient Egypt, and during the same period, weavers in other parts of the world devised techniques for making fabrics from cotton and wool threads. The Chinese discovered an even more unique source for threads and, as far back as two thousand years before Christ was born, developed a process for weaving exquisite materials from delicate filaments they unwound from silkworm cocoons.

Long before the Middle Ages, the use of woven goods for clothing had been expanded to include rugs, tapestries, and portable shelters, many of which were highly decorative. Up until the eighteenth century, however, weaving remained essentially a handcraft.

Then the "spinning jenny" was invented, to be followed a few years later by the power loom. These innovations made it possible to produce great quantities of fabrics in factories.

It has been many years then, since it was necessary for families to manufacture their own woven materials, yet the art of handweaving has persisted. It has persisted but it has by no means stagnated. Once machines eliminated the need for human hands to weave purely utilitarian materials, an impressive number of artists who are less interested in functionalism than in aesthetic expression have been attracted to the ancient craft.

This suggests that the vitality of contemporary weaving is both dependent upon and completely apart from the development of methods of mass production. Parallel movements can be seen in nearly all other craft fields. After all, machines can only duplicate, they cannot invent. And the moment a craft becomes so highly mechanized that results can be completely predictable, its very perfection

11

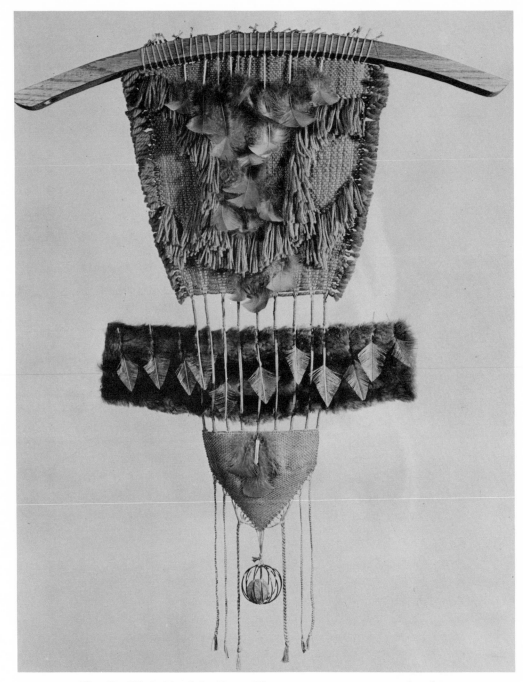

Fig. 13. "Cat's Toy," by Terry Illes, was woven on a wooden frame, using nails as stays for the warp threads. Essentially a composition of reds, it incorporates a cuff from an old fur coat, feathers, yarn scraps, and a toy her cat had abandoned. The hanging is suspended from an oak chair rocker. (Photo courtesy of the artist.)

becomes monotonous and unimaginative.

Many weavers still use a loom, of course, but a growing number are no longer content with the rigidity of loom production. By rejecting elaborate equipment in favor of simple, primitive devices, they are in intimate contact with their materials during all stages of the work, thereby becoming totally involved in the creative act.

Should these new ways of working with threads and fibers really be called *weaving?* Perhaps not, for weaving is usually defined as the art of interlacing lengthwise and crosswise fibers to create fabrics. Many contemporary hangings have no crosswise fibers at all and only in the broadest sense could be classified as fabrics. Strands are often joined together by knotting, wrapping, knitting, crocheting, braiding, or tying. Sometimes the crosswise threads are replaced by strips of wood, plastic, metal, or even by weathered twigs or branches. Bark, seeds, moss, dried grasses, fur, feathers, and other miscellaneous materials are frequently incorporated into the composition to create rich textures and colors.

It might be more apt to call these works *thread structures* or *fiber formations* instead of weavings. But whatever the nomenclature, they are exciting.

Figs. 14, 15. Canvas stretcher frames make serviceable looms for small primitive weave hangings. Following the lines of a figure 8, the warp threads are wound around opposite bars of the frame so that a ruler or strip of wood can be used as a reed to elevate alternating rows. Weft threads are carried by long needles or cardboard shuttles.

These hangings are among the first experiments of two novice weavers. The design of Fig. 14, by Lu Lundstrom, derives from elements of the sea, both real and symbolic. Driftwood and worn bits of shell are combined with scraps of variously textured yarn in greens and sandy browns.

Fig. 15, by Joan Sestak, has an earthy color scheme of black, brown, and rich terracotta. The movement created by the yarn lines and the feathers suggest flying birds and grain fields.

OPERATING A SIMPLE LOOM

Persons who knit, crochet, or embroider inevitably accumulate a stockpile of remnant threads which are too varied in size and fiber content to combine in functional items. The following projects are designed to make use of such leftovers, along with discarded toys and household rejects.

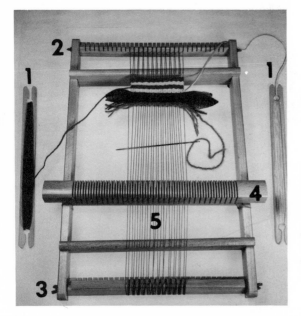

BEGINNER'S LOOM

Fig. 16. Simple table looms can be purchased for less than $5.00 and are useful for making small introductory weaving projects.
1. Thread shuttles can be made from thin strips of wood or firm cardboard. Long tapestry needles can be used for short lengths of thread.
2. The warp (lengthwise) threads are cut slightly longer than double the length desired for the finished piece. They are folded in half and hooked around the slashes in the cloth beam.
3. Each pair of threads is slipped through the slashes in the warp beam and tied.
4. They are then threaded in the movable reed by inserting one thread in a deep groove, and another in the adjacent shallow groove.
5. Warp threads.

Fig. 17. When the reed is tilted forward, every other warp thread is elevated, creating a passageway through which feathers, yarn, and the like can be passed.

KNOTTED AND TIED HANGING

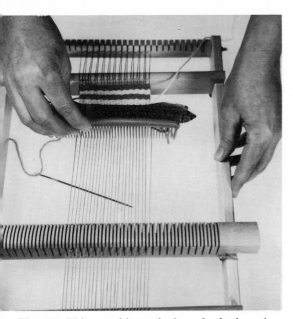

Fig. 18. Using a wide-toothed comb, the insertion is drawn back smoothly against the already woven strip. The reed is tilted backward to elevate the alternate warp threads and the weaving is continued. Wing nuts on the cloth beam can be periodically loosened so that completed sections can be rolled around it.

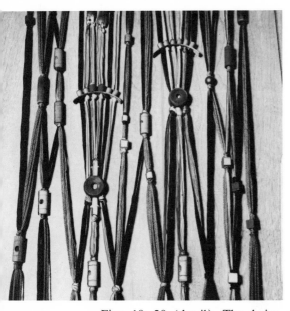

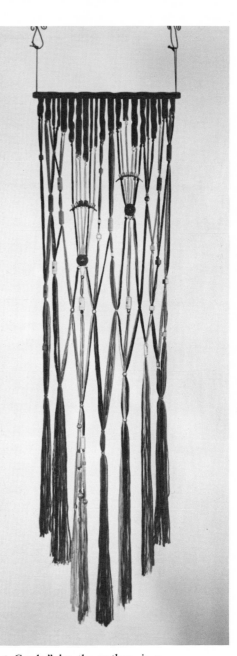

Figs. 19, 20 (detail). The design of "Lost Cords," by the author, is a composite of symbols which suggest old musical instruments and scores. Strips of charred, weathered wood form the supporting structure for cotton crochet thread and wool yarn in shades of black, brown, moss green, rose, red, and orange. Large wooden beads, salvaged Tinkertoys, pegboard separators, and arcs cut from embroidery hoops are knotted or tied into the composition.

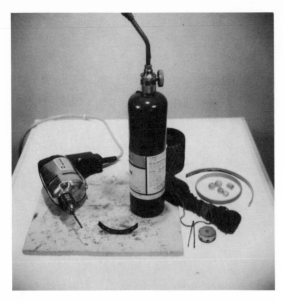

Fig. 21. Holes large enough to accommodate 25 to 30 strands of thread are drilled through Tinkertoys, beads, and arcs. (Small parts can be secured in a vise while holes are being drilled.) Some objects are painted in colors harmonious with the threads; others are charred with a propane torch. Lengths of yarn are cut about 2½ times the measurement desired for the finished hanging. A 6-inch strip of thin wire is folded in half for use as a needle.

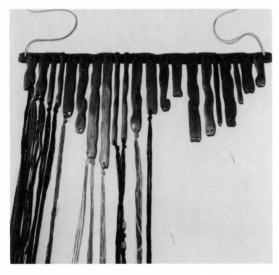

Fig. 22. Narrow wooden slats for the "keyboard" at the top are charred with the torch and scrubbed with a wire brush before drilling holes for the threads. White glue is brushed on the crosspiece, then the vertical strips are tacked in place. Bundles of 10 to 15 lengths of thread are drawn through the holes and knotted in the middle just below the wood. The threads are trimmed at the bottom when the hanging is finished.

Fig. 23. The composition is arranged temporarily before the miscellaneous elements are knotted or tied in place.
1. Knots are first looped loosely, and a nail or large needle is inserted in the loop to use as a slide to draw the knot to the desired spot. It is then tightened and the nail removed.
2. A bundle of strands is tied with a single thread, then the thread is wrapped around the knot several times. The ends are threaded in a tapestry needle, drawn through the knot, and pulled tight. A solution of 1 part white glue to 2 parts water is brushed on the ties. When it is dry, the loose ends can be clipped short without danger of raveling.

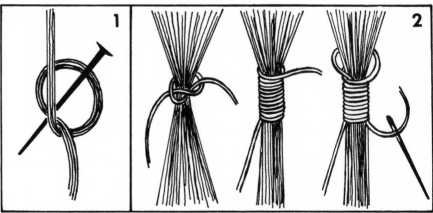

DRAWN AND REWOVEN SCREENS

The weft threads can be pulled from loosely woven fabrics, such as burlap or hopsacking, to create an openwork skeleton which can be rewoven with assorted fibers. Threads are pulled first at each end of the fabric as a guide for trimming it evenly to size. A pattern is then scaled on graph paper and the open areas marked on the fabric with chalk. (Drawn stripes should be slightly wider than the materials with which they will be rewoven.)

About 4 inches are reserved at the top for tying the screen to a length of molding, and 8 to 10 inches are reserved at the bottom for fringe. Crosswise threads are clipped at the selvage and drawn from the open areas. All of the drawnwork is completed before starting to reweave.

Lengths of ¾-inch screen-door molding are used at the top and bottom of the hanging in Figures 24 to 27; other slats range from ⅛ to ½ inch wide. Dowels, glass strips, or slats from old bamboo or plastic blinds could also be used.

Other decorative elements in the divider are scraps of yarn ranging in size from fine crewel wool to fat, furry twine marketed for gift wrapping. The weaving and tying techniques which are diagrammed are equally appropriate for such inclusions as raffia, dried weeds, strips of felt, or fabric remnants.

The drawn panel is laid flat on a large table so that reweaving can be started at the top. When it is completed, the fabric reserved at the top and bottom is fringed to within ½ inch of the rewoven areas. The top and bottom are tied to molding as shown in Figure 27 (1). The bottom fringe of the photographed hanging was made by knotting every three strands together. An alternate method of tying fringe is diagrammed in Figure 27 (3).

Yarn and slats are secured at the edges of the hanging with matching sewing thread. Several short stitches are made at the selvage, then thread is wrapped tightly around the end of the slat (or yarn) and knotted in the selvage on the other side. A dab of diluted white glue is brushed on the yarn ends before they are clipped short.

The finished screen is sprayed with Scotch-Gard, or other soil-resistant compound.

Fig. 24. This divider-screen is made from 2½ yards of brown burlap. Some of the weft threads were drawn and replaced with painted wooden slats to add rigidity, and with assorted scraps of yarn in hot pinks, reds, and orange for color and textural contrast. It can be hung from a hook in the ceiling, or suspended between two spring-tension poles. By Mary Lou Stribling.

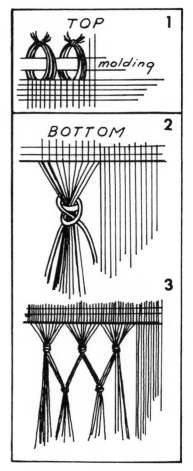

◄
Fig. 25. A closer look at the screen reveals the interesting patterns which can be obtained by tying bundles of the warp threads to the horizontal slats. Many kinds of found materials can be rewoven into such skeletons—reeds, dried grasses, raffia, fabric remnants, slats from bamboo or plastic blinds, painted strips of discarded curtain rods, rope, leather lacing, and so on.

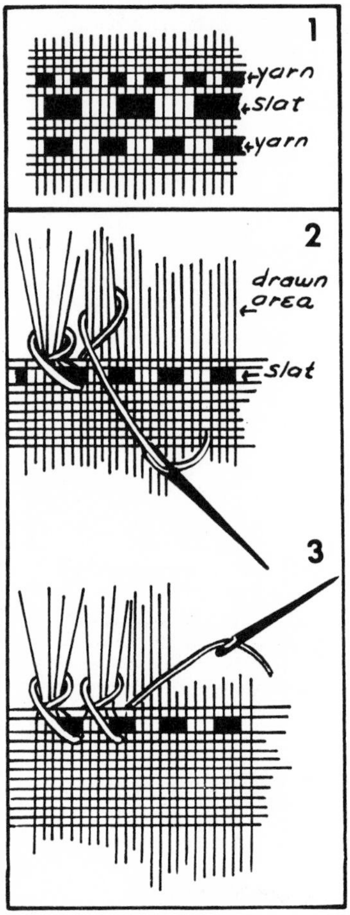

Fig. 26. 1. Where the weft threads are replaced with yarn, slats, or other inclusions, the drawn stripe should be slightly wider than the materials used for reweaving. A simple over-and-under running stitch is used.

2. Warp threads are tied to the slats by a technique similar to hemstitching. A tapestry needle is threaded with yarn, drawn under the slat and around a bundle of vertical threads.

3. The thread is brought over the slat and the loop is pulled taut. The needle is slipped back under the slat again, and the stitch is repeated across the width of the fabric.

Fig. 27. 1. The reserved fabric at the top of the hanging is fringed to within ½ inch of the rewoven area. Marks are made at ½-inch intervals across the width of the fabric, and the strands are arranged to alternate on top of and beneath the molding. They are then tied together and the ends are clipped.

2. Molding is tied to the bottom in the same manner, but instead of clipping the threads, they are knotted or tied into a decorative fringe. A burlap thread is wound several times around a bundle of warp threads and tied tightly. Using a tapestry needle, the thread is brought downward through the knot.

3. Adjacent tassels are divided in half, brought together, and tied. The fringe is trimmed evenly after ties are completed.

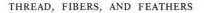

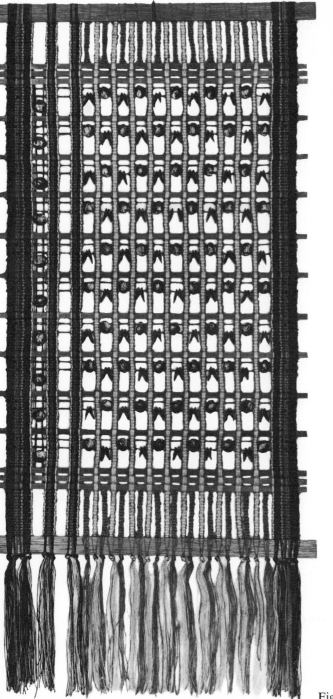

Fig. 28. Loom weaving by Evelyn Gulick. Wisteria seeds and walnut slats interwoven with linen and rayon threads. Some of the seeds were drilled to hang vertically in the open spaces; others are set in flat. (Photo by Joe Renteria.)

Fig. 29. Open-weave tapestry in black, brown, orange, and natural bouclé linen and rayon threads. Purple, dark red, rust, yellow, and tan kernels of Indian corn add texture and sharp dots of color to the composition. By Evelyn Gulick. (Photo by Ronald Lawson.)

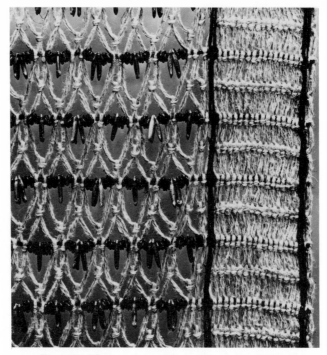

Fig. 30. Watermelon and gourd seed panel (detail) by Evelyn Gulick. The knotted open-mesh fabric is woven from black and natural linen. (Photo by Harry Crosby.)

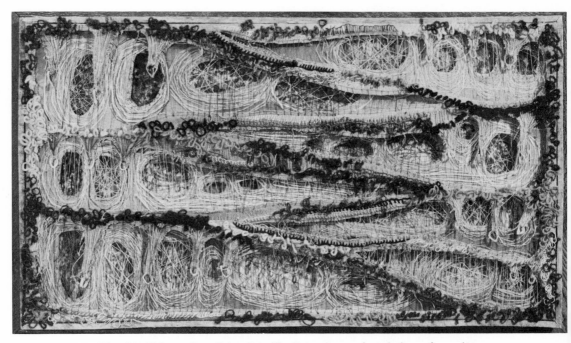

Fig. 31. "Moon Cave," by Priscilla Sage, has a foundation of overlapping scraps of colored fabrics. Found objects are enmeshed in webs of thread and surrounded by intricate masses of stitchery. (Photo by James Yarnell, courtesy of the Wichita Art Association.)

WEAVING AROUND STICKS

Mexican craftsmen are adept at loom weaving, but they have also devised many ingenious ways of creating decorative forms from oddments of thread and yarn. Their "God's Eyes," which are made from multicolored threads wrapped around crossed sticks, are becoming increasingly popular in this country for Christmas decorations.

The standing God's Eyes in Figure 32 deviate from the traditional pattern and make good beginner's projects. A three-dimensional element has been introduced by a slight change in the way the yarn is wrapped around the sticks.

The stands were made by filling paper drinking cups to different levels with plaster of Paris. The cups were peeled away after the plaster had set and the stands were allowed to dry before discarded chessmen were glued on top. Holes about ½ inch deep were drilled in the tops of the chessmen and the stands were painted flat black.

Wooden chopsticks, dowels, or strips of thin molding can be used for the supporting structure. As shown in Figure 33, when the yarn is wound to cross on *top* of the sticks, flat planes are formed. When it is reversed to cross on the *underside,* the woven area is recessed.

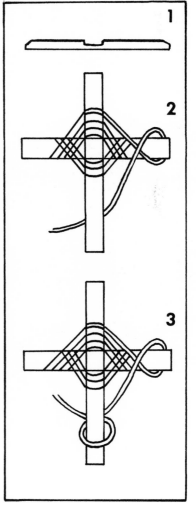

STANDING GOD'S EYES

Fig. 32. These woven decorations in hot colors are variations of traditional Mexican God's Eyes. The stands are made from orphaned chessmen and plaster. The sticks are wedged, instead of glued, inside holes drilled in the tops of the chessmen so that they may be taken apart for easy storage.

Fig. 33. 1. Flat sticks can be held together by simply gluing them at the point where they cross. A more professional method is to first carve a recess in one stick into which the other will fit.
2. The wrapping pattern is basically a figure 8. The thread is tied close to the center, carried around a stick, and brought up *over* it.
3. The thread is then carried *under the* adjacent stick and around it to make a loop on the top side. After an inch or so has been wrapped, the pattern is reversed to create the in-and-out effect shown in Figure 32.

Weaving a Thread Mobile

Childrens' toy chests are great places to forage for games and construction toys which have been abandoned because of missing elements. Discarded Tinkertoy disks are real finds, since ¼ inch dowels will fit the holes and can be used as spokes for woven wheels.

The mobile in Figure 34 illustrates several variations of the basic wrapping technique. Eight sticks, instead of four, are used on some of the forms, affording a greater variety of pat-terns. By weaving around alternate spokes on each side of the wheel, a layered effect is obtained which is especially effective with light behind it.

Lines can be spaced close together or further apart by simply winding the thread two or three times around each spoke before carry-ing it to the next. The two pieces in Figures 40 and 41 illustrate interesting possibilities for combinations of open and solid weaves. Designs of this kind are best suited for fine, tightly twisted thread or string.

Fig. 34. The combination of solid and open areas adds a new dimension to stick weaving. The forms for these examples are constructed from Tinker-toys, pushpins, and assorted buttons. They are wrapped with antique gold crochet thread.

Fig. 35. ¼-inch dowels fit the holes in Tinkertoy disks and are easily cut to desired lengths.

Fig. 36. A drop of white glue is placed on one end of the dowel, and it is firmly twisted into the hole. (Some holes may be slightly burred, necessitating a bit of sanding or hammering.) Glue is spread on the tip of the dowel, and a pushpin is added as a finial.

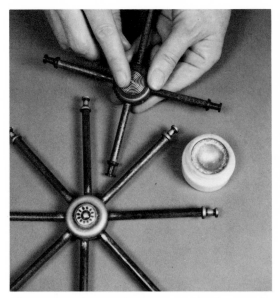

Fig. 37. Shank-back buttons are glued over the central hole in the disk, and the forms are painted to match or contrast with the threads used for weaving. For an antique gold finish, they are painted dark brown and the high spots are rubbed with wax gilt.

Fig. 38. The weaving is started by tying the thread close to the center and winding it around the spokes as shown in Figures 33 and 39. Tension is kept on the thread at all times, and it is helpful to spread a touch of white glue on the spokes as the weaving progresses.

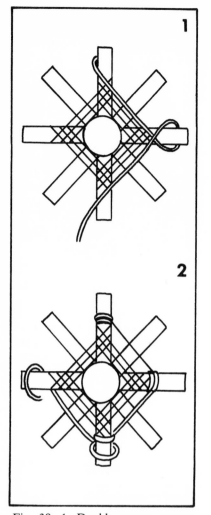

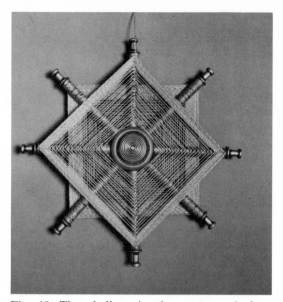

Fig. 40. Thread lines in the centers of these squares are spaced three loops apart. The solid borders are wrapped as described in Figure 39 without using the loop spacers.

Fig. 39. 1. Double woven squares are made by winding the thread around alternate spokes, then turning the form over to repeat the process on the unwoven spokes. This creates an illusion of the wheel being sandwiched in between two planes of thread.

2. For open, lacy effects, the lines are spaced farther apart by wrapping each spoke two or three times before carrying the thread to the next spoke.

Fig. 41. The border around the double squares in the center of this wheel is woven by the basic wrapping pattern in Figure 33.

Fig. 42. Large black and gold "snowflakes" woven on forms made from Tinkertoy disks, wooden dowels, and buttons. Golf tees are used for finials on the tips of the spokes.

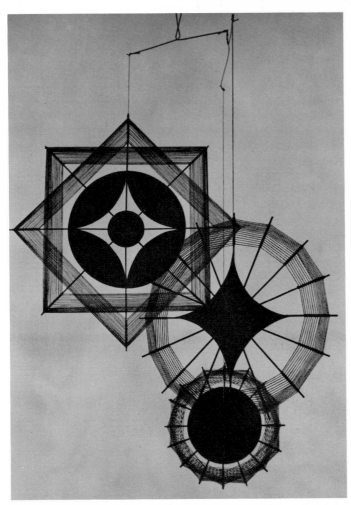

MOBILE FROM CARDBOARD AND THREAD

Fig. 43. These black line designs are so light that they stay in almost constant motion. With frontal illumination, they cast fascinating ever-changing patterns on the wall as one shape crosses in front of another.

Fig. 44. Frameworks are made from bamboo hors d'oeuvre skewers glued to shapes cut from scraps of firm cardboard. (Alternating spokes are attached to opposite sides of the cardboard.) The forms are sprayed with flat black paint.

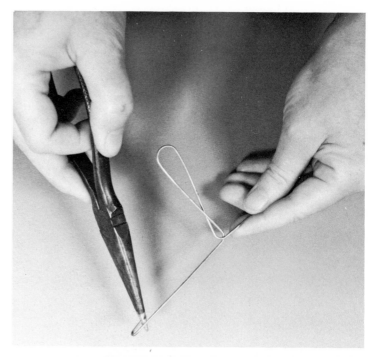

Fig. 45. A suspension is constructed from two lengths of coat hanger wire joined together with a small swivel. (See Fig. 43.)

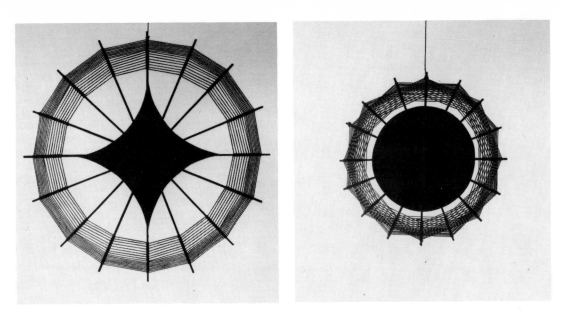

Figs. 46, 47, 48. Using a compass for accurate measurement, chalk marks are made on the spokes as guides for the first row of weaving. Spots of white glue are then placed on the marks to keep the thread from sliding. The forms are wrapped with crochet thread, using combinations of the techniques illustrated in the preceding projects.

WOVEN CLOCK

Fig. 49. The framework for this battery-operated clock is composed of square brass rods soldered to a salvaged circular saw blade. It was sprayed with alternating mists of black, red, and red-orange paint to create drifts of color that resemble copper enameling. The woven design is made from red raffia and black and gold crochet threads.

Fig. 50. STRUCTURAL MATERIALS
1. Square brass rods.
2. Circular saw blade. (The hour points are marked on the back of the saw with waterproof ink.)
3. Pattern for the hour points.
4. Battery operated clockworks.

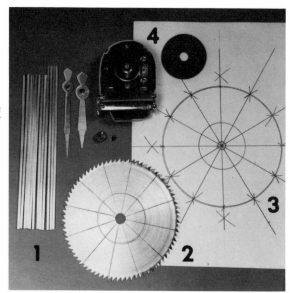

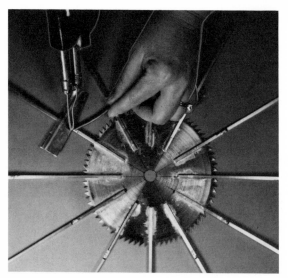

Fig. 51. The rods are soldered to the saw and carefully checked for accurate alignment. Marks for the first row of weaving are made on the rods, and a "ledge" of solder is fused on each as a stay for the threads. A strip of aluminum (to which solder will not adhere) keeps the molten solder from spreading above the mark.

DESIGNS FROM STRING AND NAILS

Nails or tacks can be hammered around the edge of a straight-sided picture frame or canvas stretcher to make a stay for woven designs from string, fibers, rope, or yarn. The thread lines can be built up in multiple layers with interweavings of several different colors and kinds of materials, or they can be used as a basic foundation for stitchery and inclusions of feathers, tassels, buttons, or dried grasses.

Experimental designs should be worked out on paper first, using arrangements of dots to represent nails, and connecting lines to represent string. In spite of the fact that thread lines between the nails are of necessity straight, they can create curved contours. To test the technique, four rows of equidistant dots are marked on paper to form a cross with arms of equal lengths and equal numbers of dots. Starting at a dot next to the center, a line is drawn to the dot on the end of the adjacent arm. From there, a line is drawn to the dot next to the center of the third arm, out to the end of the fourth, and back to the starting point. Moving out to the next-to-last dot on the second arm, then to the second dot on the third arm, the in-and-out pattern is continued until all the dots have been joined. A four pointed star with concave curves in between the rays will emerge.

This principle of winding created the inward curves on the trees in Figure 54. By varying the spacing of the dots and the lengths and numbers of the rays, many different patterns can be made.

Fig. 52. Nails or tacks can be hammered into the edge of a picture frame or canvas stretcher to make a simple stay for thread designs. It is easier to align the tacks if indentations with a nail are first made on all the placement spots.

Fig. 53. Designs do not have to be symmetrical, nor is it necessary to place nails completely around the frame. This pattern suggests trees or grasses and would make an interesting foundation for knotted compositions of feathers and odd scraps of textured yarn. It is formed by tying the string at nail 1, going around nail 2, back around nail 1 again, around nail 3, and so on. When the nails on three sides of the frame are joined, the string is carried to nail 4 and the pattern is continued.

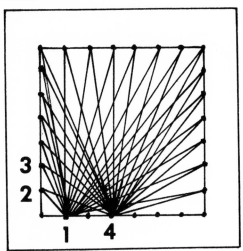

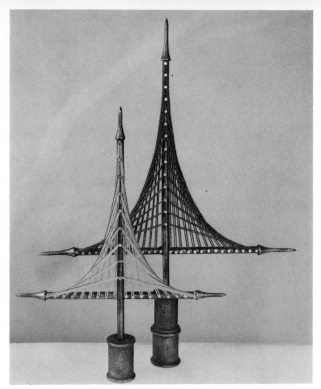

Fig. 54. Supports for freestanding tree shapes can be made from ⅝-inch wooden dowels. The vertical trunks are glued in notches carved in the centers of the horizontal bars. Golf tees, spools, and supports are painted to blend with the wrapping materials.

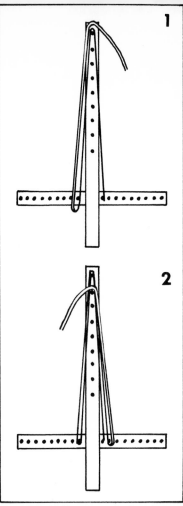

Fig. 55. 1. Starting at the tips of the bars, marks are made ¼-inch apart on the horizontal arms, and an equal number of marks are made ½-inch apart on the vertical arm. Small tacks are partly hammered in on each spot. The string is tied close to the trunk, carried around the first tack, up over the end tack on the trunk, and down around the first tack on the other side. It is then brought up over the end tack again . . .

2. . . . and around the second tack on the horizontal bar. It is carried from there over the next-to-last tack on the trunk and down around the second tack on the other side. The pattern is continued until all the tacks have been joined. Finials are then glued to the ends of the rods and the trunk is wedged in a spool stand.

◀ Fig. 56. "El Dia de la Bandera," by Bill Brewer, is assembled on a canvas-covered board. Strips of painted wood are attached with glue, and large-headed nails are partly hammered in. Heads of the nails are painted red and green and joined by lengths of colored string. (Photo by permission of Sankey Gallery.)

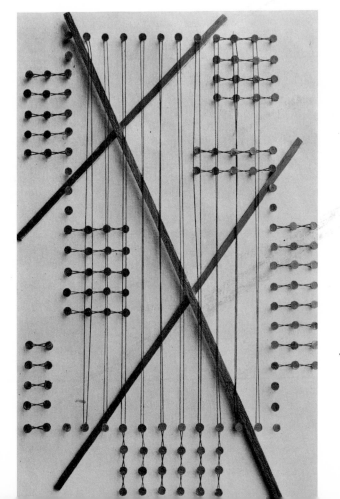

Fig. 57. "Turkish Delight," by Bill Brewer, is a collage on canvas covered with rice paper. Motifs are cut from a variety of Japanese papers, some of which are metallic, and glued to the backing. Perforations are made through the canvas for a design of colored string which is threaded through small beads and sequins and knotted on the back side. (Photo by permission of Sankey Gallery.)

Fig. 58. Christmas ornaments made from cardboard and scraps of yarn can be as warm and colorful as fine petit point. Black outlines are a distinctive touch and give the designs the brilliance of stained-glass windows.

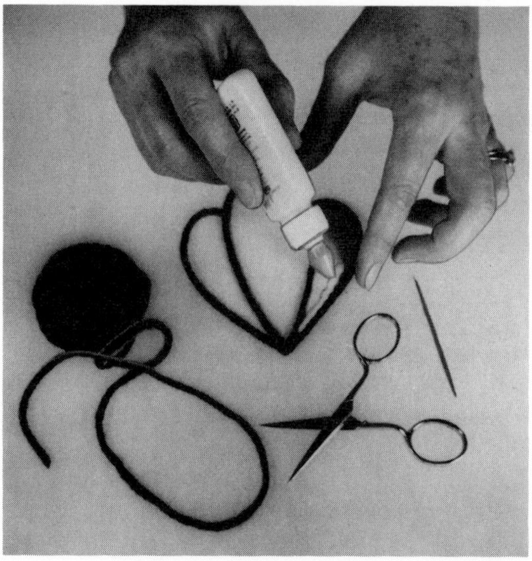

Fig. 59. Shapes are cut from firm carboard, and the edges are brushed with black waterproof ink. White glue is applied around the outline and black yarn is pressed into it, using a dampened toothpick to tamp it down. The outline is allowed to dry before filling in the rest of the design.

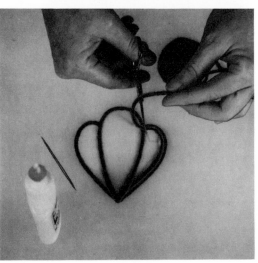

Fig. 60. The black borders are two rows wide. The yarn is snipped at corners, and the ends are pressed into the adhesive with a toothpick.

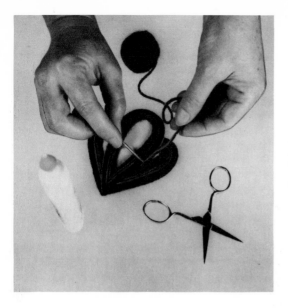

Fig. 61. The design is filled in one line at a time, then it is weighted lightly until it is dry. The process is repeated on the other side, and a row of black yarn is glued around the outer edge to conceal the cardboard form.

Fig. 62. Pins can be used to temporarily secure the yarn until the glue sets and are handy pivots at sharp turns. Ornaments can be trimmed with glued-on pompons from odd lots of ball fringe. Tassels can be hand-stitched to the bottoms.

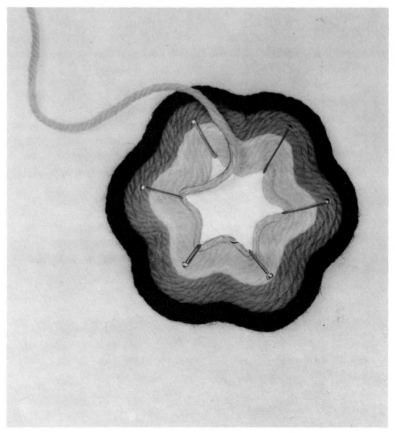

FEATHERS

We can usually find parallels between popular trends in clothing fashions and art, but it is often difficult to determine which should be given credit for instigating them. Clothing, fetishes, and ornaments have been trimmed with feathers throughout the ages, sometimes in such quantities that certain species of birds have been in danger of annihilation.

In primitive cultures, mystical significance is attached to the plumage of various birds, and feathers are an almost universal element in both their art and clothing. The color red symbolized royalty and the gods in early Polynesia, and red feathers were reserved for the garments of chieftains. Later, yellow feathers became more favored and were used exclusively for capes, cloaks, helmets, and other regalia of the ruling men. (Commoners and women were forbidden to wear them.)

Recently, there appears to have been a simultaneous revival of interest in feathers by fashion designers and craftsmen alike. Weavers in particular have recognized the textural compatibility of feathers and yarn and are combining them in works of great originality.

Happily, it is not necessary to ruthlessly slaughter birds to obtain feathers for crafts. They can be collected during the molting seasons from farmers and pet shops. Zoos are fine spots for "feather combing," sometimes yielding choice castoffs from exotic birds. Feathers from fowl which are marketed for food are also available in natural and dyed colors from craft shops.

Fig. 63. Lilinokalani cape from Hawaii. Hawaiian feather capes, cloaks, and headdresses have foundations made from a native shrub of the nettle family. The strong inner fibers of the plant were twisted into cord, then knotted to create a strong, openwork mesh. Bundles of feathers were tied to the net in overlapping rows, like shingles. Hours of painstaking labor were involved, as well as the plumage of countless birds. It is estimated that the famous cloak of Kamehameha I, which was made at the end of the eighteenth century, required half a million feathers, representing at least 80,000 birds. (Photo courtesy of the Bernice P. Bishop Museum.)

Fig. 64. "Year of the Dove," by Terry Illes, is a primitive weave hanging with yellow and white linen double warp. Feather quills are wrapped and tied to the foundation threads. This piece, as well as Fig. 13 by the same artist, was woven on a wooden frame, using nails to secure the warp. (Photo courtesy of the artist.)

Fig. 65. Mask of Kanatchu, Zuni Indians, New Mexico. Painted hide, fur, wool, and feathers. (Photo courtesy of the Brooklyn Museum.)

Fig. 66. An exquisitely crafted pinched ceramic form is the foundation for this contemporary mask by Dominic DiMare. Waxed linen thread was laced vertically through perforations in the fired clay, then woven into an intricate pattern of crosswise threads, knots, and small beads. The airiness and graceful linear movement of cassowary feathers (collected from a zoo) contrast pleasantly with the disciplined order of the basic structure. (Photo courtesy of Henry Gallery, University of Washington.)

Figs. 67, 68. Fragments can be snipped from colored feathers and assembled into decorative plaques. Gessoed and painted wooden plaques are used here for backings, and the inner tips of the feathers are set into thin smears of white glue. Fig. 67 has a circle of gold leaf beneath the flower and is trimmed with colored chenille twists. The flower in Fig. 68 has a melted glass nugget in the center, surrounded by bands of glued yarn.

chapter 3

Fabrics and Papers

History does not tell us which came first—weaving or sewing. Garments were fashioned in some ancient cultures by tying or knotting strips of woven fabrics together, but there is evidence that even more primitive people who had not yet learned to weave knew the basic principles of sewing.

The first needles were "found," rather than formed, and consisted of lengths of bone, shell, or wood with convenient holes for carrying threads made of plant fibers, tendons, or strips of hide. Needles today are designed for an incredible range of specialized tasks. Aside from their obvious relationship to the manufacture of clothing and household furnishings, they are essential for all kinds of surgery, from the uninvolved suturing of a simple cut to the highly sophistocated process of organ transplants.

It was inevitable that the arts of weaving and sewing would be accompanied by the art of patchwork, for it is impossible to cut into a length of fabric without creating scraps which are too precious to throw away. Also, garments often go out of style before they wear out and have a way of becoming faded and threadbare in one spot before the rest of the material shows signs of deterioration. Along with the thrift involved in reusing these discards, they have sentimental associations which add another dimension to the pleasure of working with them.

Patchwork was an essential craft in early America. Unlike weaving, which was often participated in by every member of a family, the task of transforming scrap fabrics into useful items was primarily relegated to women. There were two basic types of design: *appliqué,* utilizing a foundation to which scraps were attached, and *piecework* where scraps were stitched together, eliminating the need for a foundation. But these techniques were simply beginnings for the skilled seamstress. She added such a profusion of elaborations that bedspreads and quilts gradually became elevated from household necessities to treasured works of great elegance.

Fig. 69. "Star of Bethlehem," or "Rising Sun," appliqué and pieced-work quilt, made by Mary "Betsy" Totten (1781–1861). The one-patch pattern of 648 pieces is bordered by appliqué work in polychrome floral glazed cottons. (Photo courtesy of the Smithsonian Institution.)

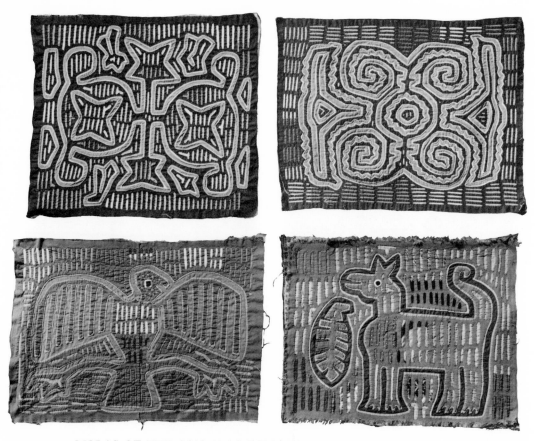

MOLAS OF THE SAN BLAS INDIANS

Figs. 70, 71, 72, 73. Scraps of all kinds of cotton fabrics are used for colorful appliqués by the Indian women of the San Blas Islands, Panama. At the very least, they rank as high-level folk art, and many examples fully justify classification as fine art. Although more decorative than functional, "molas" were fashioned into blouses by joining two together at the shoulders.

The designs are not created by the usual method of stitching patches on top of a foundation sheet. They are made by a "reverse appliqué" technique in which layer upon layer of fabrics are pierced to expose underlying materials. The openings are meticulously turned under and secured with almost microscopic stitches.

Early patterns, such as those shown here, were traditional, and usually related to their folklore. Some of the designs which appear to be simply abstract patterns are actually symbols from their religion. Others are derived from plants, reptiles, animals, and birds, both real and imaginary.

Recently, the women have begun to include elements copied from modern magazines, cigarette packages, and can labels. Since they are unable to read and understand the meanings of the symbols and letters they find decorative, their combinations are often indescribably humorous.

By the middle of the nineteenth century, the art of patchwork was enthusiastically pursued by women in all economic levels. Many beautiful quilts and coverlets were made for the sheer joy of creation, without any intention that they should actually be used. On special occasions they might be displayed on a guest's bed. Usually, however, they were discreetly removed before the bed was occupied and whisked back into cedar scented storage chests, there to remain until another visitor provided an excuse for airing them.

For the most part, patterns were traditional and were identified by traditional names long after the original meaning of the name had been forgotten.

A number of factors contributed to the decline of homemade quilts in the twentieth century. The active and inquisitive young urban homemaker of the 1920's and 1930's was savoring her emancipation from much of the drudgery formerly attached to raising a family. She no longer needed the sociability of the quilting bee, and she did not *have* to make her

Fig. 74. "Rose of Sharon," appliqué quilt probably made in the third quarter of the nineteenth century. The work is distinguished by its fine diagonal quilting and unusual stuffed-work motifs. (Photo courtesy of the Smithsonian Institution.)

Fig. 75. Pieced-work quilt of the late eighteenth century. It includes scraps of embroidered linen and a toile thought to commemorate the Treaty of Pillritz (1793), the first formal alliance in opposition to the French Revolution. (Photo courtesy of the Smithsonian Institution.)

own bedcovers. But beyond that, the traditional patchwork patterns were simply not compatible with her changing tastes in home furnishings.

For thirty or forty years, patchwork was regarded as a rather old-fashioned activity for elderly people and rural "country folk." Then in the 1960's, something remarkable happened. A few imaginative designers suddenly turned their talents toward updating the old concepts. They devised faster methods of production by combining machine stitching with freer, less tedious techniques of hand embroidery. But more importantly, they stirred the musty air of traditional design with the fresh breeze of originality. Flaming with color, vibrating with textural enrichment, needlework literally exploded into the world of creative crafts with a burst of energy that will continue to propel it forward for many years to come.[1]

The fuse of this explosion was *design,* for innovations in materials alone could not account for the force of the movement. However, since these innovations have made it possible to work faster, therefore more spontaneously, they are entitled to a share of the credit.

SPECIAL PRODUCTS FOR APPLIQUÉ

Certain new products have special significance to the needlecraftsman. The old laborious process of basting each part of an appliqué in place before stitching it permanently is now largely unnecessary. The reverse side of appliqué patches can be simply sprayed with adhesive, arranged on the foundation, and smoothed down. This provides an opportunity to study the composition and make any necessary changes, since the pieces can easily be peeled off and repositioned.

Casein-based fabric adhesives are marketed in bottles with applicator tips. They are stickier and less fluid than ordinary white glues and are extremely useful for making decorative yarn pictures and hangings. The adhesives are not permanent enough for items which will be subjected to frequent washing, but they are still very convenient for temporarily securing a row of yarn before couching it with thread.

Of even greater potential, perhaps, is the development of a sheer, flexible plastic material which can be heat-fused between layers of fabrics for permanent lamination without sewing. Although it is not recommended for certain synthetic fibers or lightweight whites, it broadens the possibilities of decorative appliqués, while at the same time eliminating the tedious chore of basting and hemming.

For example, fabrics which are too soft to use as a foundation can be laminated to a firm base of canvas, buckram, sailcloth, and the like. Scraps for the decorative pattern can be heat-bonded to one side of the plastic, cut to shape without the danger of raveling, then permanently steam-bonded to the foundation. The plastic filaments are so delicate that they add no bulk and are completely invisible between the layers.

Surprisingly enough, by carefully controlling the heat, this material can also be used for paper appliqués.[2]

FABRIC COLLAGE

Many contemporary craftsmen have completely disassociated patchwork from sewing, approaching it instead as a type of collage, or pasted-down assemblage. This work requires only a sheet of pressed board or plywood, glue, and an accumulation of scrap fabrics.

Where fabrics of different weight and naps are combined, a single adhesive is not always sufficient and it is a good idea to experiment with several to determine which will provide the best results. The white glues are probably

---

[1] Diagrams of various kinds of stitches used in contemporary stitchery can be readily obtained from many new books on the subject, as well as from department stores and shops selling needlecraft supplies. However, persons who are already acquainted with basic embroidery will find it even more stimulating to invent their own decorative stitches.

[2] Spray adhesives, fabric glues, and plastic laminating materials are listed in the Index of Supplies.

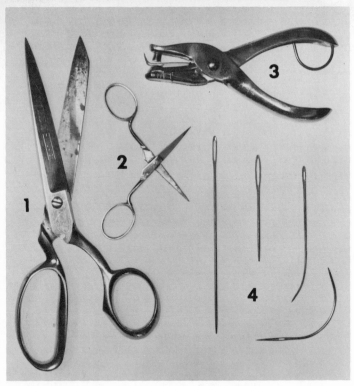

Fig. 76. BASIC TOOLS FOR WORKING WITH FABRICS AND PAPERS
1. Dressmaker's shears.
2. Pointed embroidery scissors.
3. Paper punch (for fabrics, paper, and lightweight cardboard.)
4. Needles for specials purposes. Left to right: long tapestry needle for weaving, knotting, and stitchery on open weave fabrics; book-binder's needle for thick fibers and heavy materials; packing needle for lacing or couching with string; curved needle for upholstery, padded materials, and so on.

Fig. 77. Recent innovations in sewing supplies have greatly simplified fabric appliqué. One such product consists of a web of polymerized fibers temporarily attached to a paper backing. The underside of appliqué scraps are bonded to the plastic with a hot iron, then the shapes are cut out.

Fig. 78. The paper backing is peeled away and the motif is ready to be steam fused to the fabric foundation. Decorative stitching around the edges of the appliqué is optional but is recommended for items which will be washed frequently.

Fig. 79. "Shining City," by Charlotte Patera, is made of scraps of satin, velveteen, crepe, and printed cotton in purples, reds, olive, and rusty brown. Gold braids, assorted sequins, and beads are used for accents. Some parts of the design are softened by overlays of sheer voile. The materials are attached by zigzag machine stitching and simple hand stitches.

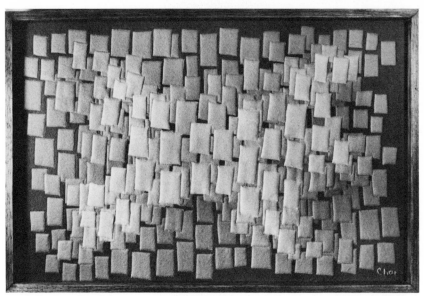

Fig. 80. "Sunglow" is a composition of felt scraps in a subtle range of sunny colors—pale yellow, lemon yellow, cadmium yellow, yellow orange —superimposed on a yellow ochre background. The design is built up in layers, working from dark to light shades. By Charlotte Patera.

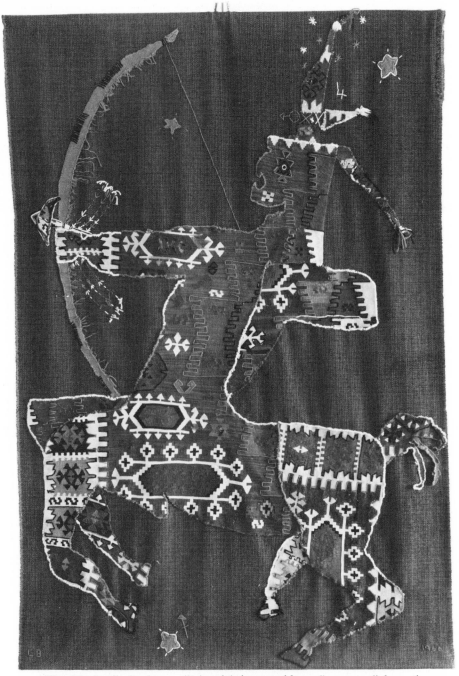

Fig. 81. Lucile Brokaw calls her fabric assemblages "cousages," from the French verb, *coudre* (to sew). Assorted materials are selected for color and surface quality and are meticulously put together by hand. Her subject matter ranges from the mystical and whimsical, to the tragic and ironic. "Sagittarius" is a large hanging measuring 78 × 52¾ inches. (Photo courtesy of Adele Bednarz Galleries.)

the most versatile, as long as they are applied thinly so that they will not soak through the cloth. It is difficult to keep them from staining delicate silks and sheers, and these are best attached with a good paste glue or spray adhesive. The casein-based fabric glue mentioned earlier is less likely to spread into surrounding areas than white glue, and is an excellent choice for additions of yarn, braid, cording and the like.

On certain types of collage the fabrics are deliberately saturated with adhesive to produce a waxy, impervious surface. Matte acrylic medium was used on the fabric-covered bottle in Chapter 7. The same technique can be followed on flat compositions.

Experienced designers often work spontaneously without drafting a preliminary design. It is safer for the novice to first work up a simple color sketch, enlarge the linear pattern to scale, and transfer it to the backing. Fabric scraps in random shapes can then be arranged experimentally to evaluate the compatibility of textures and colors.

It is easy to become mesmerized by the at-tractiveness of the materials themselves, and be tempted to use only the most beautiful pieces, regardless of how they go together. This can result in a design as monotonously irritating as a recording with the volume turned up too high.

The beginner may find it helpful to make a few experimental designs from assorted scraps which have a single common denominator—color. For illustrative purposes, let us assume that the color is red. The scraps can run the gamut of the red family from hot orange reds to cool blue reds, and should include dark shades and light tones along with prints and solid colors. When the scraps are spread out on a table, discordant pieces can be rejected, and dark neutral added—black, gray, or brown. The composition is then restricted to these ingredients.

This is perhaps an overly disciplined working method, but it is one way to become more sensitive to harmonies and contrasts in textures and values, and to be less concerned with the actual fabric than with what it contributes to the design.

Fig. 82. "Greek Island." Fabric collage by Jean Varda.

Fig. 83. "MB #8" is part of a "mod bod" series of collage paintings by Laura Devendorf, which incorporate teasingly anatomical forms with abstract linear patterns. Natural linen, paisley printed fabric, and segments cut from egg cartons are glued to canvas and combined with thin washes and thick impastos of paint. (Photo by Jim Kean.)

Fig. 84. "Song of the Arabian Nightingale." Mixed-media collage by Bill Reily. (Collection of the Marion Koogler McNay Art Institute, San Antonio.)

PAPERS

Papers and fabrics have a closer affinity than might immediately be evident, and some products are even made from the same raw materials. They also have a certain visual compatibility which makes them natural companions in many kinds of compositions.

The word paper is derived from papyrus, a pithy reed which the ancient Egyptians sliced and pressed into a writing material. However, the process upon which our modern methods of manufacture are based was invented in China by Ts'ai Lun in the year A.D. 105.

Ts'ai Lun's first papers were made from the inner bark of the mulberry tree in much the same way that tapa, a nonwoven cloth, was made by the early Polynesians.[3] Later, the

[3] Tapa making is described in Chapter 10.

Chinese learned to make a better product from a pulp of salvaged rags, rope, twine, and other fibrous materials.

Through the years, scientists in other countries have continued to improve the process of papermaking by such refinements as disintegrating chemicals, wood pulps, dyes, and machinery. Paper is now produced in such a staggering variety and quantity that we are prone to take its existence for granted, and overlook the fact that it is one of civilization's small miracles.

Paper As an Art Medium

It is generally assumed that Ts'ai Lun's interest in papermaking was motivated by his desire to find a good writing material, but we cannot separate Oriental writing from art. Chinese calligraphy could be called a form of "picture writing," with each symbol exquisitely executed to tell its part of a story as gracefully as possible.

The early illuminated manuscripts were equally decorative. Although we can surmise that certain symbolic and illustrative designs were incorporated with letters and words to make the text more meaningful, many elaborate embellishments were added just to make the pages beautiful.

With the inventions of movable type and engraving plates, printing and illustrations could be reproduced mechanically, thereby isolating them for a period of time from the art of hand painting. In a unique fashion, the collagist has brought them back together again. Newspapers, musical scores, magazine ads, and other "machine-made pictures" become vehicles for art works in the same way that pastels or oil paints are vehicles for painting. And like reused fabrics, scrap papers may retain some elements of a previous life charge which lend a subtle energy to the work.

The collages of Braque, Picasso, and Gris represent some of the outstanding contributions of the Cubist movement to modern art. They inspired a generation of imitators before significant innovations in the medium emerged.

The strange, dreamlike collage-montages of Nick Nickolds, Figures 87, 88, 89, 90, demonstrate an interesting approach to the use of found papers. They are distinctly surrealistic, but the photographic images inject a disturbing realism into scenes which are not real at all, except, perhaps, during times when the subconscious becomes a positive force. The artist's thoughtful analysis of his concept is equally provocative: "Collage is a unique medium for persons in their search for self, since it is free from the restrictions of other art forms which demand a prolonged education in technique. It is more a tool for intimate expression than public demonstration. Perhaps it is really closer to a new form of writing than painting."

Experimenting with Paper

Paper collages can be made on sheets of firm cardboard if a paste-type adhesive is used. Thin cardboard is inclined to warp or buckle from more fluid adhesives, and it is safer to use white glues or acrylic mediums on backings of plywood or pressed hardboard, preferably coated with gesso.

Some papers will stretch and wrinkle from

Fig. 85. "Guitar and Wine Glass" by Pablo Picasso. Pasted paper and charcoal. (Collection of the Marion Koogler McNay Art Institute, San Antonio.)

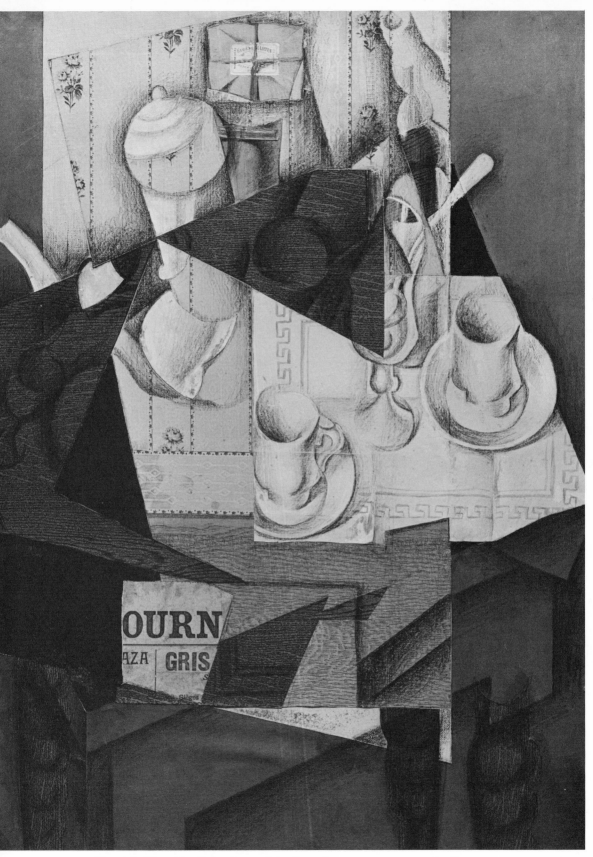

Fig. 86. "Breakfast" by Juan Gris. Pasted paper, crayon, and oil on canvas. (Collection of the Museum of Modern Art, New York, acquired through the Lillie P. Bliss bequest.)

Fig. 87. The collage-montages of Nick Nickolds have the hallucinatory quality of dream visions. Although the separate elements are ordinary subjects cut from colored magazine photographs, they are combined in a manner that produces pure fantasy. Like many of the artist's montages, "World of the Mushroom" has been reproduced for large scale posters.

Fig. 88. "Ultimate Boon" (detail), from the Hero's Cycle. Nick Nickolds precuts a large amount of diverse material from books and magazines, selecting whatever catches his eye and imagination. Sorting through his stock, he discovers that the pictures fall naturally into categories of color, texture, or subject matter, from which poetic or philosophical statements gradually arise. (Photo courtesy of the artist.)

Fig. 89. "Descent from the Cross" (detail). Collage, according to Nick Nickolds, is a "typewriter for the subconscious," and a medium for writing visual poetry. He glues his compositions to pressed hardboard coated with a gesso ground, using a heavy printing brayer to eliminate air bubbles and wrinkles. (Photo courtesy of the artist.)

Fig. 90. In the process of reproducing some of Nick Nickold's collages, inks are tested for color intensity by running trial printings on scrap papers or rejects. As shown by this detail, sometimes the superimposed images are so interesting that they become new compositions entirely different in character from the original works.

moisture unless the tension between wet and dry surfaces is equalized after they are coated with glue. This can be done by tamping the paper against the backing with a soft sponge dampened in a diluted solution of the adhesive. Care should be taken not to damage the surface quality of the paper by rubbing it. Certain coated papers, including those used for slick magazines, are especially susceptible to abrasion.

Interesting effects can be obtained from combinations of scrap papers and dried leaves, pressed flowers, raveled string, bits of fabric, broken mirrors, and even such exotic materials as feathers and butterfly wings. Adhesives should always be pretested, as well as different methods of application. Generally, the adhesive for fragile materials should be applied to the foundation and the materials flattened against it with a soft cloth. Dried leaves and flowers are easier to handle if they are first slightly dampened between sheets of moistened blotters. String, rope, and other springy fibers are more tractable if they are presoaked in thin wallpaper paste or diluted white glue.

Charcoal, inks, crayons, or paints can sometimes serve to delineate certain areas of a collage or to pull the composition together. (See Figures 84, 85, 86.) The acrylics are excellent for this purpose since they dry quickly and can be diluted or thickened for transparency or opacity.[4]

These new plastic emulsions have led to many remarkable changes in art materials, particularly in the field of painting. They can be used on almost every kind of surface for effects ranging from translucent washes, similar to water colors, to heavy impastos which resemble oil paints. (They should not be applied over surfaces which are greasy, or have been previously coated with oil paints.)

Although the initial cost of acrylics is about double that of poster paints, they go further, are waterproof, and are highly resistant to fad-

ing or discoloration. They can be thinned with water or thickened with gels. Varying degrees of surface shine can be controlled by the addition of mat or glossy acrylic mediums. The mediums are also excellent sealers.

There are a number of ways of pretreating scrap paper to alter its character without completely obscuring it. One of the simplest is to arrange assorted objects, such as keys, leaves, washers, string, or bits of screening, on newspaper or colored magazine pages and spray them lightly with paint. When the paint is dry, the objects can be moved and resprayed to overprint delicate images on the original pattern.

The manner in which paper is fragmented adds a special flavor to the finished work. Crisply defined pieces are obtained by cutting; pieces with softly blurred edges by tearing. Distinctive fragments can also be produced by charring.

The working area should be free of drafts, and it is best to use fairly heavy paper. The paper is dampened on both sides with a sponge, cut or torn into random scraps, and the edges are held against a candle flame until they are scorched. When the paper burns, it can readily be blown out, but it is wise to keep a shallow pan handy for dunking a piece which gets out of control. Veil-like deposits of soot can be added by holding the paper at an angle above the flame. They must be sprayed with fixative before using them in a collage, however, or the soot will smear.

After the paper is dry, burned particles are brushed away, leaving brown-rimmed serrated edges. If necessary, the fragments can be smoothed with a warm iron.

Another method of charring paper has some limited value for producing special shapes or motifs. The motif is preplanned to a certain extent by folding a square or circle of dampened paper into eighths or sixteenths before burning the edges. The flame is allowed to eat deeply into some parts of the outline and in spots along the folds. From time to time the paper is unfolded to study the shape and de-

---

[4] Plastic paints are generally referred to as "acrylics," but some manufacturers have stated that it would be more accurate to call them *polymers*.

cide where additional charring might improve it.

The motifs may be combined with uncharred cut or torn fragments. Unique designs can be created by superimposing several charred motifs from patterned paper in graduated sizes, using shapes of solid colors in between them.

Candle drippings on brightly colored magazine ads or illustrations will form free, spontaneous patterns and textures. The wax is spattered at random on the paper, then the entire sheet is brushed with water color or thinned acrylic paint. When the paint is dry, the sheet is respattered with wax and brushed with a wash of dark brown or black ink. The wax is removed by ironing the paper between several layers of paper towels. Speckled patches of both the original printing and the first coat of color will be exposed.

A *tjanting,* which is a tool designed for drawing wax-resist patterns on fabric batiks, can be employed in a similar fashion to create "scribble and doodle" designs on paper.[5] Candle stubs, wax crayons, or paraffin is melted

[5] See Index of Supplies.

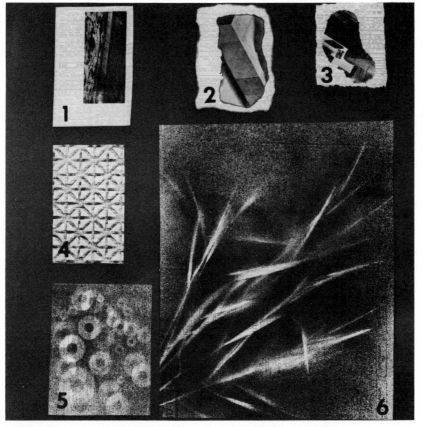

Fig. 91. FRAGMENTED AND PATTERNED PAPERS FOR COLLAGE
1. Cut fragments.
2. Charred fragments.
3. Torn fragments.
4. Pattern on newspaper resulting from a black crayon rubbing of an aluminum grill.
5. Pattern on newspaper resulting from a scattering of washers sprayed lightly with black paint.
6. Shadowy images on newspaper resulting from an arrangement of grasses sprayed with black paint.

◀ Fig. 92. Motifs burned from magazine pages.

Fig. 93. WAX-RESIST PATTERNS ON NEWS-PAPER

Using a tjanting, melted candle wax was trailed in random scribbles over newspaper, then brushed with a thin wash of green acrylic paint. When the paint was dry, other scribbles and splashes were added and brushed with a wash of brown acrylic paint. The dried paper was placed between paper towels and ironed to remove the wax.

in a can set in a pan of water on a hot plate. The tjanting is dipped into the hot wax and the pouring spout is wiped with a paper towel. The spout is then placed against the paper and used as a sketching instrument. If the wax congeals before the tjanting is empty, it can be reheated by holding it over an alcohol lamp. A candle flame will also reheat the wax, but it will leave a soot deposit on the spout which must be wiped off or it will leave a stain on the design.

When the paper batiks are ironed, the wax penetrates the fibers and causes them to become beautifully translucent. Aside from their suitability for collage, sheets of paper decorated by this process can be framed for screens or window decorations, or be fashioned into lamp shades.

Fig. 93. Paper Batik.

Paper for Decorations and Creative Play

Although paper can be easily torn, shredded, burned, or cut, its basic ingredients are extremely durable. Properly sealed for protection against moisture and insects, it will last indefinitely. But since it is discarded in such vast amounts, we are provided with an ever-ready supply of no-cost materials which are as suitable for temporary decorations as they are for permanent art works.

It would be difficult to find a more diversified medium for "creative play" than paper.

And often in the process of constructing some unpretentious project which has no aesthetic purpose beyond providing a spot of color for a dark corner the germ of an idea is born which can be expanded into more ambitious work.

Figs. 94, 95. Cut paper designs are a relatively new Polish folk art dating from the latter half of the 19th century. Although these examples are quite intricate, the technique can be simplified and adapted to many kinds of found papers.

Early Polish patterns were silhouettes of one color intended for wall decorations. Now they are made of several layers of multicolored papers. Colors and combinations of motifs vary according to the preferences and skills of individual craftsmen, but the characteristic style is traditional. The foundation of the design attached to the large tray in Figure 94 is cut in one piece from black paper. Two to four layers of colored cutouts are superimposed on top of it. The smaller motifs in Figure 95 are used to decorate furniture, household items, and note papers.

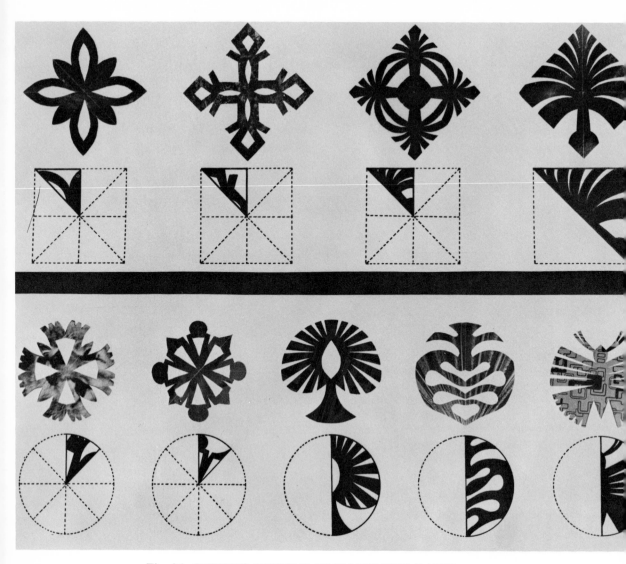

Fig. 96. CUTTING DESIGNS FROM FOLDED PAPER

It is is easier to design decorative motifs with scissors and paper than to draw them with a pencil, and often, delightfully unexpected things happen. These examples were cut from magazine pages by folding squares and circles as indicated in the patterns, and cutting out the solid figures. The last two designs in the top row were cut exactly the same, but by folding one square into eighths and another in half, entirely different pictures were produced.

The plastic laminating material shown in Figs. 77, 78 is especially useful for paper appliqués of cutouts of this kind. Like fabric motifs, the paper is heat-fused to the plastic before it is cut. Tests should be made to determine the proper temperature for the iron and the reaction of the backing to heat. (A cover sheet of tissue should be placed on top of the cutouts to protect them from direct contact with the iron.) These designs were bonded to smooth construction paper with the iron set on "rayon."

Fig. 97. The triangular backing for this decorative panel is ⅛-inch pressed hardboard painted flat black. The design was cut from scraps of assorted wrapping papers in solid colors, prints, and metallics. The trunk was attached first by brushing a thin film of white glue on the backing, then tamping the paper into it with a moistened sponge. Other parts of the design were built up a section at a time. When the panel was dry, it was sprayed with several coats of satin finish varnish.

Fig. 98. Paper cutouts can be attached directly to a wall for permanent or temporary murals. For temporary decorations, the backs of the attachments can be brushed or sprayed with rubber cement, or the papers can be glued to a sheet of transparent self-adhering plastic before they are cut. Permanent decorations can be secured with wallpaper paste or white glue. Leftover remnants of patterned self-adhering plastic can also be used for murals.

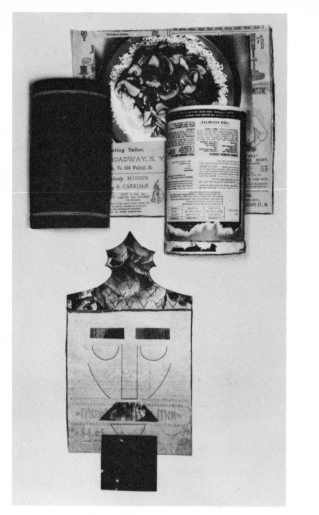

Figs. 99, 100. DECORATIVE MASKS FROM PAPER

99. The king in Figure 100 is composed of the materials shown in the upper part of Figure 99. A pattern was drawn first to fit around the halved cereal carton, and the face was cut from a reproduction of an old newspaper. (The newspaper was sprayed with a mist of gold paint.) Crown, eyebrows, moustache, and beard were cut from magazine ads and glued on the face. The face was then slashed on the black lines so that sections could be folded out as shown in the finished example.

100. The mask was glued to the vertical edges of the carton, using spring paper clips to hold it in place until the adhesive had dried. For classroom experiments masks can be left flat, using the foldouts alone for three-dimensional effects.

101. Colorful flowers are easily made from magazine papers and the printed patterns add a great deal to their fanciful characteristics. Buttons, large beads, slices of bottle corks, or pompons cut from ball fringe can be used for centers and fillers.

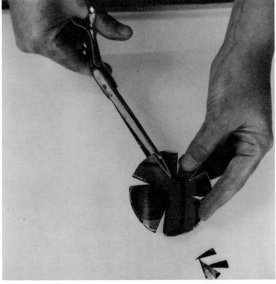

102. Any number of shapes are possible, but simple fringy blossoms are most effective. Three circles of graduated sizes are used for patterns. 15 to 20 layers of paper are cut in the largest size and the edges are notched. 10 layers are enough for the smaller circles.

103. The circles are pierced with a nail, and the papers are threaded on lengths of florists' wire. One end of the wire is bent to serve as an anchor, and for extra dimension, the layers are separated by small beads. The flower head is secured by stringing a pompon on the stem and gluing it to the back of the largest circle. The center is glued on last.

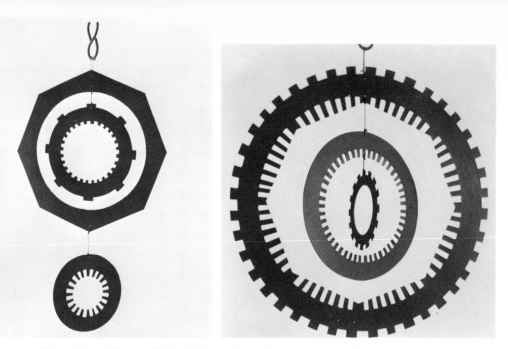

Figs. 104, 105. CARDBOARD MOBILES

These mobiles have the appearance of wrought iron, but the more practical weight of cardboard. They can be suspended from a steel needle hammered into the ceiling. Any kind of firm cardboard will do, including used file separators and cartons. A sharp X-Acto blade will insure clean cuts, and any burrs left on the edges can be removed with fine sandpaper. (For a more rugged iron-like texture, the cardboard can be stippled on both sides with gesso paste.) The forms are sprayed with flat black paint and strung on black thread so that the parts turn independently.

Figs. 106, 107. CHRISTMAS ORNAMENTS AND PENDANTS

106. Scrap cardboard is also useful for ornaments and seasonal decorations. Unique patterns for basic forms can be created by folding paper in half and experimenting with combinations of straight and curved cuts. Edges and both sides of these examples were coated with black acrylic paint, then bright scraps of felt, small pieces of mirrors, and felt disks cut with a paper punch were attached with white glue.

107. The cardboard foundations used here were covered with felt instead of paint to make pendants which are durable enough to be worn during the holiday season. Mirrors, felt scraps, and bits of yarn were used for the decorative patterns. Shapes cut from tin cans can be dyed in brilliant colors and substituted for both cardboard and mirrors. (Dyed tin is described in Chapter 4.)

Papier-Mâché

Papier-mâché can be used in two forms: *pulp* and *strip*. Absorbent papers are best and for layered strips it is hard to top a time-worn favorite—newspapers.

It is easier to work with fragmented papers if only small amounts at a time are saturated with adhesive. Large batches are likely to disintegrate into a pulp before they can be used

Fig. 108. Necklace from balls of papier-mâché pulp, dyed seeds, and tiny wooden beads. The pulp was rolled into balls of graduated sizes and pierced with a toothpick. When they were completely hard, they were dipped in hot fabric dyes along with the seeds. Dark red, bright red, and orange acrylics were dry-brushed on the high spots. The finished necklace was coated with matte acrylic medium.

Fig. 109. "Minnie," by Jackie Curry, is made of papier-mâché and assorted sewing scraps. The head began as a ball of crushed newspaper molded into shape with a layer of aluminum foil. After building up the face with small wads and strips of newspapers soaked in wheat paste, cotton cable cording was glued on for hair. Rolls of soft cardboard cut from egg cartons were covered with papier-mâché for arms and legs. Head, arms, and legs were coated with gesso modeling paste and colored with acrylic paints. The pink sateen casing for the doll's body was stuffed with strips of discarded nylon stockings. Pieces of a straw place mat and coarse lace were dampened and shaped over a light bulb to form the hat. Several coats of white glue were brushed over it to insure rigidity.

up. Wallpaper paste is the classic binder, but white glue diluted with equal parts of water makes a very hard, durable product. The drippy problem of excess adhesive can be reduced by soaking the strips in a shallow pan, then placing them in a sieve or collander over the pan to drain. They can then be smoothed on a selected core until the desired number of overlapping layers has been built up.

The size and arrangement of the paper fragments will determine the texture of the finished piece. They can be smoothed on in random patches, or in vertical or horizontal rows. The completed shell will be absorbent and should be sealed with gesso or acrylic medium before it is painted. A final coat of medium or dull sheen varnish will protect the finish and give it a lustrous polish.

chapter 4

Scrap Metals

Metalworking is not really ancient in relation to the history of man himself, but since certain aspects of it have been known in widely scattered parts of the world for thousands of years, it can hardly be called new.

Native copper, silver, and gold were the first metals to be worked because they were soft enough to be readily shaped and were deposited in some abundance close to the surface of the ground. Scientists believe that the Egyptians had a rudimentary knowledge of iron nearly nine thousand years ago, but its evolution from primitive to sophisticated production followed a sporadic, uneven course.

Even in the more highly developed societies, iron has been in general use for less than three thousand years, yet it is awesome to contemplate the changes it has made in our lives. It was a vital force in the so-called "Industrial Revolution" in the 1700's which marked the transfer of manufacturing from the human hand to the machine. But the development of cheaper, more efficient ways to produce steel

(an iron alloy) in the mid-1800's was the catapult that hurled the civilized world into the Machine Age.

Steel is not indestructible. It can be eroded by chemicals or prolonged exposure to natural elements. However, the ever-swelling accumulation of discarded steel objects along our roadsides is evidence that it will last a very long time, even when it is abused by neglect.

To the conservationist, these discards are a continuing source of dismay and, indeed, even the most dedicated junk enthusiast condemns the thoughtlessness of the litterbug. Nevertheless, the clutter exists and treasures are there for the taking—cans, hub caps, wheels, rusty hulks of automobiles, abandoned camping utensils—which need only a bit of cutting and rejoining to become artistic masterpieces.

Well, perhaps not *all* of the resurrections are truly masterpieces. In fact, such an intention would be both inhibiting and pretentious, and would serve as a sobering brake on exuberant creativity.

69

Fig. 110. "Where Will All the Young Men Go?" Pierced metal helmet by Ronald Griffiths. (Photo by permission of Anima Mundi Gallery.)

Exuberant creativity is not necessarily associated with humor or whimsicality, though certainly these qualities are evident in many examples shown here. But the crusty, pierced helmet by Ron Griffiths in Figure 110 conveys a grim and chilling message, and the powerful form by Marcus White in Figure 111 suggests a terrifying machine for death and destruction. There is even something elusively sinister about the owls by Lino Pera in Figures 133 and 134, arising, perhaps, in the first piece from the foreboding watchfulness of the creature's deep, hooded eyes; in the second, from the tense attitude of a hunter who has marked his prey.

However, the very conception of these works involves aspects of primitivism which were discussed in the first chapter. There is further a common disregard for conventionality, as well as a rather disconcerting directness and a scorn for the cliché.

CONCEPTS OF DESIGN

The examples in this chapter demonstrate three different approaches to creating art from found materials. In the first, the previous life of the materials remains very present and has a direct bearing on the message of the work.[1] In the second, characteristic shapes, colors, or textures of the found materials have influenced, possibly even inspired the design, yet their identities as specific objects may not immediately be evident.[2] In the third, the original form and function of the materials are totally disregarded. The artist evaluates them objectively in terms of raw materials which are abundantly available for little or no expense.[3]

All of these concepts are valid and it is doubtful that any artist represented here con-

[1] See Figs. 110, 111, 112, 115, 118, 122.
[2] See Figs. 113, 114, 116, 117, 139.
[3] See Figs. 143, 165, 166.

sistently adheres to a single philosophy or deliberately designs by an inflexible format. Per-

sons who do so are likely to prefer a medium
which is less adventuresome.

Fig. 111. Sculpture from welded car parts by Marcus White. (Photo
courtesy of the artist.)

Fig. 112. Ball joint relief by Marcus White. (Photo courtesy of the artist.)

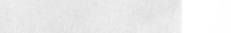
Fig. 113. Steel pipe, cut apart and reassembled by welding. By Marcus White. (Photo courtesy of the artist.)

Fig. 114. "Club Ladies" by Lino Pera. Assorted brass objects bolted together.

Fig. 115. "Headache" by Lino Pera.

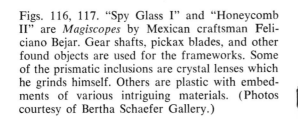

Figs. 116, 117. "Spy Glass I" and "Honeycomb II" are *Magiscopes* by Mexican craftsman Feliciano Bejar. Gear shafts, pickax blades, and other found objects are used for the frameworks. Some of the prismatic inclusions are crystal lenses which he grinds himself. Others are plastic with embedments of various intriguing materials. (Photos courtesy of Bertha Schaefer Gallery.)

Fig. 118. High-school student Howard Glick built his lively "Charioteer" from springs, large nails, bolts, wire, automobile spark plugs, and miscellaneous hardware. Parts are soldered together. (Photo courtesy of Contemporary Gallery.)

Figs. 119, 120. Ronald Griffiths' "Aztec Hub Caps" originated from junked automobiles. The perforations were made with a welding torch, resulting in rolled, irregular edges which contrast richly with the silvery glint of the base metal. Candle cups are attached behind the disks. (Photos by permission of Anima Mundi Gallery.)

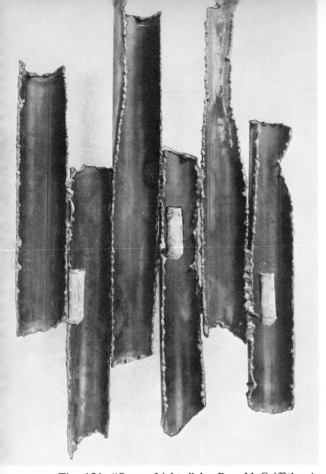

Fig. 121. "Organ Lights," by Ronald Griffiths, is a wall candelabrum. Parts were cut with a welding torch from automobile drive shafts. (Photo by permission of Anima Mundi Gallery.)

Fig. 122. Art Grant's "Etruscan Warrior" was once a brass loving cup. The cup was separated from the base, then inverted on top of it and secured with liquid solder.

TOOLS FOR WORKING WITH METAL AND WOOD

Fig. 123.
1. Hacksaw, equipped with replaceable blades for wood or metal.
2. Tungsten carbide abrasive rods are designed to fit a hacksaw frame and can be used to slice dense materials, such as ceramic tiles, bricks, or glass bottles.
3. Scroll saw.
4. Claw hammer.
5. Tack hammer.
6. Ball peen hammer.

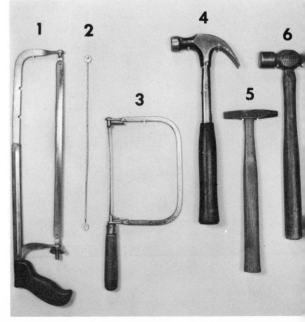

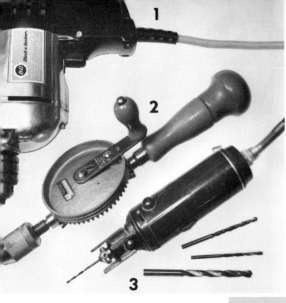

Fig. 124.
1. Electric drill.
2. Eggbeater hand drill.
3. Lightweight electric hobby drill and assorted bits.

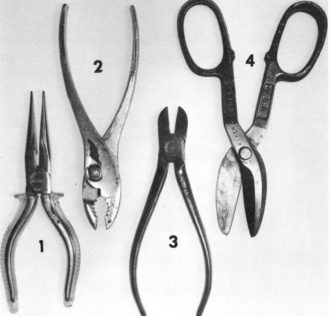

Fig. 125.
1. Needle-nosed pliers.
2. Blunt-nosed pliers.
3. Wire cutters.
4. Lightweight metal snips.

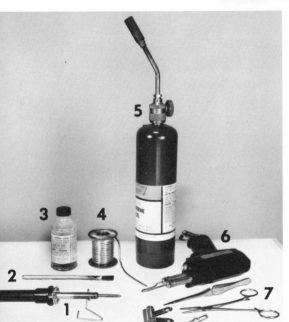

Fig. 126.
1. Hobby iron for soldering wire and lightweight metals.
2. Bristle fluxing brush.
3. Acid flux.
4. Acid-core solder.
5. Propane torch.
6. Soldering gun. (Available with interchangeable tips designed for special jobs.)
7. Metal paper clips, alligator clamps, self-locking tweezers, and hemostats, for holding small parts together while they are being soldered.

SOLDERING

Metals can be soldered with either an iron or an inexpensive propane torch, but many jobs can be accomplished so much more efficiently with a combination of the two tools that the extra expense is justified. This is particularly true of sweat-soldering, where the iron can be used for tinning small parts and temporarily securing laminations, and the torch used for smoothing out the solder and bonding the structure into a single, strong unit.

Soft-soldering is adequate for most projects and can be used for lead, tin, brass, copper, and the assorted alloys from which keys, coat hangers, washers, nails, junk jewelry, and clock parts are made. It cannot be used for aluminum.[4]

The first step in soldering is to thoroughly clean the metal parts. This not only means removing dirt, rust, corrosion, and grease, but also any protective coatings of paint, varnish, or lacquer. Thin films of lacquer on coat hangers and brass objects can usually be buffed away with steel wool. Heavier deposits of paint, such as printed matter on cans, are most quickly removed by blistering the paint with a torch before polishing off the flakes with steel wool. A wire brush and a strong solution of detergent and hot water will take care of oily matter which would prevent the solder from bonding with the base metal.

Soft solder is a compound of lead and tin which melts at a lower temperature than the metals it bonds together. It is available in a number of different forms, but acid-core soldering wire is probably the most versatile.

Acid flux is a "liquefying agent" which lowers the melting point of solder so that it flows more freely. It is highly corrosive, and should be treated with respect. Precautions will be noted on the containers of all materials of this na-

ture, and they should be carefully observed.[5]

Fluxed objects should be scrubbed in a soapy solution immediately after soldering is completed to prevent discoloration. A final bath in a weak solution of vinegar and water will counteract any remaining traces of acid.

Soldering with an Iron

Steps in Soldering with an Iron

1. The metal parts are cleaned.
2. The iron is heated and the tip is scrubbed with a wire brush until it is shiny.
3. Liquid or paste flux is applied to the metal joint and to the tip of the iron.
4. A droplet of solder is melted onto the tip of the iron to "tin" it, and excess solder is shaken or brushed off. The metal is then heated by the iron.
5. A stick of solder is brought to the joint and a tiny bead is melted away. The iron is rubbed over the metal until the solder flows smoothly into the crevice. More flux is added if the solder rolls into a ball instead of spreading.

The novice is always inclined to use too much solder. It should be considered a kind of glue, not a filler, such as grout or mortar.

The steps in flame-soldering are essentially the same as described for an iron except that the metal is first heated with a medium-hot flame, then it is fluxed and reheated. Snippets of solder can be arranged on the seam with tweezers and melted with the torch, or the solder can be dabbed against the hot metal to leave a deposit of small beads. (Except where there is a deliberate intention to flood or plate an entire area, the solder should not be held in the flame.) The flame is played over the joint only long enough to completely liquefy the solder. If prolonged heat is applied, both metal and solder may deteriorate.

An asbestos pad should always be placed under work being torch-soldered.

---

[4] For information on hard-soldering, brazing, or welding, the reader should consult books which treat the processes in detail. A few titles are recommended in the Appendix.

[5] Acid-core solder and acid fluxes should not be used for soldering electrical parts.

Sweat-Soldering

Laminations of cutout metal shapes, thin metal sheets, or multiple overlays of assorted flat objects should be *sweat-soldered,* meaning that a thin film of solder is fused in between the layers, and not simply around the edges. Although sweat-soldering can be done with either a torch or iron, it is greatly simplified when both tools are used.

Steps in Sweat-Soldering with a Torch

1. The metal parts are cleaned and placed on an asbestos pad with surfaces to be soldered upward.

2. Flux is brushed over the metal. The torch flame is turned about medium high and played over the metal until it is hot. The surface is dabbed lightly with the tip of a stick of solder until it is stippled with tiny dots. (Small objects, such as washers and clock parts, will require only one or two dabs.)

3. Another coat of flux is applied, then the flame is played over the solder until it flows into a thin, even film. This is called "tinning."

4. The base layer is heated, fluxed, and the upper lamination is positioned on top of it with tinned side down. The flame is played over the sandwich until the solder is melted. An icepick or old fork may be used to keep the laminations from sliding out of alignment until the solder has solidified.

On multiple laminations, the heat must be carefully controlled on each new addition to minimize repeated reliquification of the solder between the lower layers.

SWEAT-SOLDERED PENDANTS

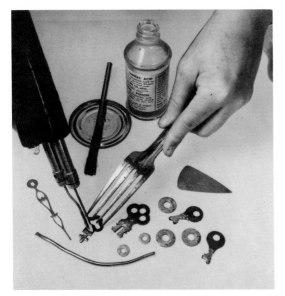
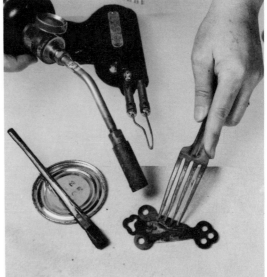

Fig. 127. Designs for jewelry from found objects can seldom be worked out on paper. It is best to experiment with arrangements of the materials themselves. After a selection is made, the metal parts are cleaned and the undersides of the laminations are fluxed. A soldering iron is used here to tin a clock hand, keys, and brass washers on the spots where they will be attached to the copper form at the right.

Fig. 128. The copper form is placed on an asbestos pad. The keys are refluxed and positioned on the base with tinned sides down. The soldering gun is set aside and a propane torch is used to melt the solder between the layers of the metal "sandwich." (The use of two soldering implements is optional for small laminations.) An old fork is handy for keeping the parts in proper alignment until the solder has solidified.

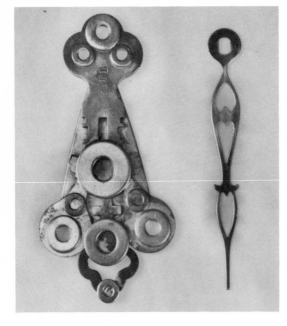

Fig. 129. Oxidized particles are washed from the pendant with soapy water. It is then dried, fluxed, and the washers set in place on top of the keys. They are carefully heated with the torch flame just to the point where the solder liquifies. Following the same procedure, the brass clock hand is attached last.

Fig. 130. Three layers of flat steel keys and four tiny washers were sweat-soldered on a small square of tin to create the cross on the left. Wheels from an old clock were soldered in the center to conceal the foundation. Steel parts were darkened with gun blue and buffed with fine steel wool.

The rococo pendant on the right appears to be constructed from intricate silver and gold cutouts, but it was made entirely from steel keys, washers, and brass clock parts. The largest keys form the foundation; smaller keys were arranged to overlap and bond together the parts of the first layer. Washers, clock hand, and tiny cogwheels were soldered in place last. For a patina of antique silver, the pendant was washed with black acrylic paint, and the high spots were polished with a soft cloth.

All three pendants were sprayed with transparent plastic to prevent tarnishing.

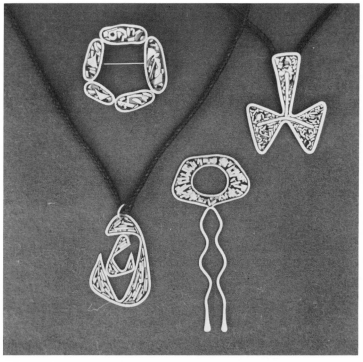

Fig. 131. The process of cutting out jewelry forms inevitably results in an accumulation of random scraps. Some jewelers reclaim the metal by melting it into castings. Bob Storm's ingenious solution is to sweat-solder silver fragments into mosaic inlays for brooches, pendants, earrings, and hair ornaments.

Decorative Soldering

A different kind of flame-soldering is used chiefly for decorative, rather than functional purposes. It is essentially a process of tinning an entire surface with a thick deposit of solder, either to change its color or to fill and smooth imprinted numbers or legends on such objects as keys and can lids. The surface is heated, fluxed, and liberally dotted with snippets of solder about the size of a wooden match head. Heat is applied until the solder flows into a solid sheet.

Fascinating textures can be created by dropping filings or tiny snippets of solder on an *unfluxed* surface, then heating them only to the point where they bond to the base but remain elevated in irregular splashes and rivulets. The elimination of flux is important, since it would flatten and spread the trails of solder. Also, as described later in the chapter, heat from a torch flame creates beautiful colorations on certain metals. With the application of flux, the patina is eradicated.

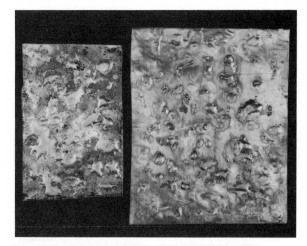

Fig. 132. DECORATIVE SOLDERING. Pieces of unfluxed tin (left) and copper (right) were heated with a torch, then dabbed with a stick of solder to melt away droplets of various sizes. The flame was played over the solder just long enough to bond it to the base. With unfluxed solder instead of acid-core wire, raised patterns will be more sharply pronounced.

PATINATING METALS

The scarcity of detailed information about coloring found metals indicates that patination is not an exact science except where all factors are known, including the precise nature of the metals involved. Metals are rarely used in a pure form, and found metals can be made from innumerable alloys which are usually rather loosely classified as bronze, brass, tin, steel, iron, or copper, according to how they look or respond to soldering.

Actually, in a collection of brass gears, washers, keys, screws, and bolts, which may be of identical color, some will have a larger proportion of copper or zinc than others, and some may even contain small amounts of tin or lead. Bronze objects can be made from various mixtures of copper and tin, and there is no way to determine whether or not other metals have been added to make them harder or more malleable. To further complicate the picture, we may discover that we are working with imitation metals. Not infrequently, junk-shop finds which appear to be bronze or brass may really be composed chiefly of tin or iron alloys with surface washes of unknown derivation.

It is understandable then, that a number of found materials will react to chemicals in unexpected ways, and it would be foolish to flatly state that chemical X will turn them green or brown. Also, the average craftsman is prohibited from fully exploring the possibilities of patinations because many processes require chemicals which are both difficult to obtain and extremely dangerous unless they are handled under laboratory conditions which provide safeguards against burns and toxic fumes. Such processes have not been included in the following experiments, nor have dozens of other tests which were judged to be of insignificant value as far as Found Art is concerned.

Some of the chemicals used are poisonous or corrosive and precautions are noted in the instructions. However, a number of supplies which are common to every household are equally dangerous, including insecticides, ammonia, certain detergents, bleaches, grease dissolvers, and toilet bowl cleaners. It is assumed that the reader will keep these materials beyond the reach of children and will observe any warnings listed on their labels.

In addition, the solutions should only be used where there is adequate ventilation. An exhaust fan over the working area is an excellent investment. As an alternate, I recommend working in a shady spot outdoors.

Figs. 133, 134, 135. This parliament of owls by Lino Pera demonstrates how a single subject can be portrayed in many different ways with gears, pipe joints, and other salvaged objects. The artist uses a saturated solution of ammonium chloride to develop antique green patinations on parts of his bronze and brass sculptures.

All metals will become patinated in one way or another if they are exposed to weather for a period of time. But since the required period may be a decade or so, it is more practical to resort to techniques for aging them artificially.

It should first be understood that coloring metals by natural or chemical oxidation is not related to coloring objects with paint. When certain chemicals are applied to metals, they start to etch or erode the surface. On alloys containing a large percentage of iron, this is usually a destructive process in which particles of metal disintegrate into rust, or iron oxide. Where alloys contain a large proportion of copper, the patination is not destructive. Instead, the chemicals combine with elements of the metals and form minute crystals of various colors. With fast-acting agents it is possible to actually watch this taking place, and it is fascinating to observe the growth of the crystalline patches under a magnifying glass.

Gradually, the patches spread until they link together into a scaly skin. This may take time, however, and repeated application of the chemical solutions. Also, the crystalline color will not be evenly distributed as would a coat of paint. Part of the characteristic beauty of oxidized metal derives from the subtle changes in both color and textural crust.

At first, the patina may be powdery and can readily be rubbed off. If it is left undisturbed for a week or so it becomes part of the metal itself and can be removed only by extensive grinding or polishing.

Reactions which are noted in the experiments are those that were considered to be most useful. None of the tests produced identical results, though in some cases they were fairly close. In several instances, colors were affected by the method of application.

To add a few general observations, the best solutions for antiquing keys and assorted steel objects were found to be heat and oil (Test No. 2), and gun blue (Test No. 3). Other treatments simply created profuse reddish-brown or black rust. It is well to be aware of

these responses for they indicate that unless rust stains are acceptable on constructions composed of a variety of metals, steel, soldered joints, and iron inclusions must be protected with varnish or lacquer before treating the piece with chemicals. The ochre-brown rust which formed on some of the washers in Sea Garden, Figure 139, combines pleasantly with the blue green patina of the brass materials, but similar reactions on other pieces have been most unattractive.

Chemical oxidation of tin has been largely unexplored in the craft world and some of the experiments revealed beautiful possibilities. In a number of cases, rich browns and iridescent greys emerged without the accompanying grittiness associated with rust. Where rust occurred, there was a remarkable color range from yellow ochre to burnt sienna. It was possible to stabilize them by gently washing away loose particles and coating the metal with dull-sheen varnish.

In order to evaluate the reactions of the colorants on different metals, several identical objects were used in each test. These were: pennies, brass washers, tooling copper, copper jewelry forms, steel locker keys, and strips of tin cut from unlacquered cans. In addition, such objects as watch parts and small handmade bells from India were included. (The latter were labeled "brass," but their reactions indicated they had merely been pigmented to look like brass.) Silver, gold, and other precious metals were not tested.

All metals to be colored should be thoroughly precleaned to remove grease or protective finishes, then buffed with fine steel wool.

The experiments begin with readily available materials and progress to chemicals which are less commonly used. Manufacturers are noted in the Index of Supplies. Other brands of equal merit may be ordered through hardware stores and pharmacists, or obtained from chemical supply houses.

Volume measurements are not as accurate as weight measurements but they are included for persons who do not have gram scales. To keep the solutions as close as possible to the test batches, spoons should be filled lightly to the brim without packing and leveled with a knife blade.

The worktable should be protected with plastic film and several layers of newspapers or paper towels. Aluminum foil or other metal materials should not come in contact with the objects being tested, and the solutions should not be mixed in metal containers.

Experimenting with Metal Colorants

1. PROCEDURE: Metals are arranged on an asbestos pad and the flame of a propane torch is played over them until color develops. When cold, the objects are sprayed with dull-sheen varnish or lacquer to keep them from darkening with age.
OBSERVATIONS: Judged most effective on tin and copper, which take on beautiful iridescent rainbow tints. Copper becomes vividly colored with shades of red, purple, yellow, and orange. Tin colors are chiefly cool, ranging from lavender to deep blue.
2. PROCEDURE: Metals are coated with a film of linseed oil or machine oil, arranged on an asbestos pad, and heated as above. (Heavy coats of oil may burn briefly.)
OBSERVATIONS: Tin and copper colors are slightly more subtle than in test No. 1. Steel (on keys tested) aquires a velvety dark-to-tawny-brown patina.
3. PROCEDURE: With a cotton swab, metals are liberally coated with gun blue (available in hardware stores), and recoated after five minutes. When the color appears even, they are rinsed under running water without rubbing the metal. They are allowed to set overnight before buffing the high spots with a soft cloth or very fine steel wool.
OBSERVATIONS: An excellent simple method for antiquing steel, brass, and copper. Keys become bluish-black; brass and copper turn varying shades of cool brown. Patina is easily scratched immediately after treatment, but is quite durable after it has hardened.

4. PROCEDURE: A paper towel is saturated with vinegar, the metals are arranged on it and vinegar is brushed on exposed surfaces. The process is repeated periodically for several hours before allowing the objects to dry.
OBSERVATIONS: Subtle iridescent blue and rose markings are formed on copper. Changes were insignificant on other metals.
5. PROCEDURE: Metals are placed in a covered jar or a nonperforated plastic bag and sprinkled with sawdust saturated with vinegar. The bag is shaken to make sure all surfaces are buried, then closed tightly. Coloration progress is checked after 24 hours.
OBSERVATIONS: After 24 hours, small bright blue-green crystals start to form on copper and brass, but periods of three days to a week may be necessary before significant changes come about. To retain the crystals, objects are rinsed gently in water and allowed to dry before spraying them with lacquer or varnish. If crystals are brushed off, a stippled iridescent pattern of blues and browns will remain.
6. PROCEDURE: Metals are arranged on paper towels and painted with a saturated solution of table salt and water (about 1 teaspoon salt to 1 ounce of water). The towel is slid into a nonperforated plastic bag and a jar lid filled with household ammonia is placed beside it. The bag is closed tightly. After about an hour, the metals are rewet with the salt solution and the bag is resealed. When coloration is successful, metals are rinsed gently and allowed to air dry.
OBSERVATIONS: An excellent process for obtaining brilliant turquoise colorations on brass and copper. Patina is delicate for a week or so and should not be handled.
7. PROCEDURE: Using the process in Test No. 6, a solution of 23 grams (4 teaspoons) cupric sulfate to 2 ounces of water is substituted for the salt solution.
OBSERVATIONS: Brilliant shades of cobalt blue and purple appear quickly on copper and brass. As it dries, the color changes to greenish turquoise. Mottled red-brown oxides form on

tin. (Cupric sulfate is poisonous. Precautions on the labels must be observed.)

8. PROCEDURE: With a cotton swab or old brush, metals are coated with undiluted muriatic acid. They are recoated in about an hour, and after twelve hours are rinsed gently under running water and left undisturbed for several days.

OBSERVATIONS: Greenish crystals form on copper, light yellow green crystals form on brass, and soft yellow ochre oxides form on tin. Tin colors can be stabilized by dusting off the loose powder and spraying them with lacquer or varnish. (Muriatic [hydrochloric] acid is used to clean tiles and masonry and is generally available in hardware stores. It is highly corrosive and even in closed containers can cause rust on tools and other metal objects within a range of three feet. Rubber gloves should be worn to protect the skin, and the acid should be used only in a well-ventilated area.)

9. PROCEDURE: Following the process described in Test No. 8, after twelve hours the metals are recoated with muriatic acid. After several hours they are rinsed under running water.

OBSERVATIONS: When the muriatic acid is reapplied, the green colorations and iron oxides are removed. Copper retains a marbleized pattern of pale yellow and black. Tin is satinized and takes on a silvery gray patina with rosy undertones.

10. PROCEDURE: Metals are arranged on newspapers or paper towels and exposed surfaces are brushed with a solution of 25 grams (7¼ teaspoons) ammonium chloride and 4 ounces of water. The solution is reapplied severel times over a perioid of five or six hours. Objects are then rinsed under running water and air dried.

OBSERVATIONS: Bright green crystals form on brass and copper, becoming a softer green after several days. Steel and tin objects rust profusely. Patina is delicate until it has aged for several weeks.

11. PROCEDURE: Following the process in Test No. 10, a solution of 7 grams (1¼ tea-

spoons) cupric sulfate, 3 grams (1⅛ teaspoons) ammonium chloride, two ounces of water is substituted.

OBSERVATIONS: A handsome antique green patina forms on copper and brass. Pennies and certain other copper alloys may have marbleings of yellow green. Tin reacts to the solution almost immediately and turns blackish brown. If washed at once, a bronzy patina remains. If exposed to the solution repeatedly, rich redbrown oxides are created. Tin should be washed, gently patted dry, then sprayed with varnish or lacquer.

12. PROCEDURE: A pea-sized lump of sulfurated potash (or liver of sulfur) is dissolved in 5 ounces of boiling water. The hot solution is brushed on metals until a velvety black crust appears. Objects are immediately washed and rubbed gently to remove excess deposits. When dry, the high spots are polished with a soft cloth, or buffed with fine steel wool.

OBSERVATIONS: An excellent method for antiquing copper and silver, but not recommended for steel or tin. Weaker solutions, using 10 to 15 ounces of water will produce iridescent slate blue and rose tints on copper. (Sulfurated potash is poisonous and the fumes can be toxic. Use only in a well ventilated area. Solutions deteriorate quickly and after about 8 hours may not be useable.)

13. PROCEDURE: A solution of 25 grams (7¼ teaspoons) ammonium chloride, 12 grams (2½ teaspoons) crushed sulfurated potash, 8 ounces of water is brushed on metals until a black deposit forms. Metals are washed immediately and patted dry.

OBSERVATIONS: Dark gunmetal blue and brown markings are formed on copper.

14. PROCEDURE: Metals are arranged on a paper towel and slipped into a nonperforated plastic bag. An open container of the solution in Test No. 13 is placed beside them and the bag is closed tightly.

OBSERVATIONS: Within a short period, sheet copper takes on iridescent shades of slate blue. Pennies and assorted copper objects may also acquire rosy tints.

Fig. 136. Interesting spiky medallions which resemble burrs, flower sepals, or sea anemones can be made by soldering nails and staples to washers or bits of tin.

Fig. 137. The points on staples are extremely sharp and should be trimmed with wire cutters. The finished medallions here are attached to circles cut from can lids and have brass and steel washers in the centers. Stems will be made from coat hanger wire, nails, or fine brass tubing. Before assembling them on a permanent base, it is wise to experiment with temporary arrangements on a block of styrofoam.

Fig. 138. Nails and other metallic parts of the design are patinated by the process in Test No. 10. Several pieces of weathered driftwood are glued together for a base, and the shortest elements are hammered into place. Small steel, brass, and copper nails are secured first, then large nails, some of which have caps of washers and brass nuts.

Fig. 139. Holes are drilled in the base to fit the stems of the larger medallions, and epoxy glue is used to seat them firmly. The gray driftwood has faint markings of worn blue-green paint which blends pleasantly with the turquoise and warm rust-brown colors of the metal. "Sea Garden" is by the author.

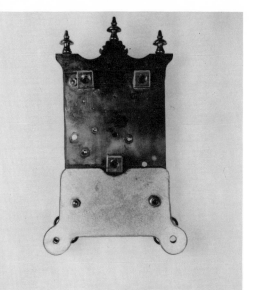

Fig. 140. The design of the back plate from a defunct 400-day clock suggests a crown, and with the addition of a few keys and other parts from the clock, a humorous royal portrait can be constructed. Several tentative arrangements of the objects were tried before they were finally soldered as shown in Figure 142.

Fig. 141. The construction was then turned over, and three large nuts were soldered on the back to elevate it slightly above the backing.

Fig. 142. A scepter was made for "Little King" from the clock's winding key, a cogwheel, and a section of copper tubing. Two perforated clock parts serve as his collar. The highly polished brass required several different chemical treatments before the surface was sufficiently etched to take a good patina. The solution in Test No. 11 was used first. After several days, loose powder and rust were brushed away, and the crown, eyes, nose, scepter, and collar were patinated by the process in Test No. 10. The face was darkened slightly by a thin wash of brown acrylic paint, then the entire piece was coated with matte acrylic medium. By Mary Lou Stribling.

TIN CANS

Tin is long overdue for a promotion in craft status. When it is properly designed and finished, it is every bit as beautiful as more precious metals, and for many purposes it is far more appropriate.

Sheet tin in several gauges is available in hardware stores, but an unlimited supply can be salvaged from empty cans at no cost whatever. (*Tin* is actually a misnomer for both of these products since in nearly all cases they are made from steel and merely coated with a thin layer of tin.) Cans are especially useful for decorative projects, a fact which Mexican craftsmen have apparently recognized since the first can was discarded.

Pierced Designs

It is a simple matter to place flat tin sheets or cut motifs on a pad of newspapers and perforate them with nails, chisels, or other sharp instruments. However, cans must be supported upon a core of some kind to keep their walls from becoming deformed under the pressure required to pierce them.

Wax serves this purpose admirably and can be used over and over. Candle stubs or paraffin are melted in a can set in a pan of hot water over a hot plate. The can to be pierced is filled to the brim, and refilled as the wax congeals and shrinks. When the core is completely hard, a pattern is marked on the can with waterproof ink. The can is then placed on a padded surface and pierced.

An impact center punch will greatly facilitate the piercing operation, and can be purchased in stores carrying hardware and sheet metal supplies. This little instrument is designed along the lines of a fat, stubby ball point pen. When its point is placed directly on the metal and the other end is pressed firmly downward, an inner point is activated by a strong spring and darts out to punch a dimple in the metal. Once the entire design is dimpled, it is easy to complete the perforations with nails or an electric drill.

The core is melted out by placing the can upside down in a larger can set in a pan of water over a hot plate. The remaining film of wax is scrubbed off in hot soapy water.

For decorative containers that will hold water, indented designs can be made with the impact center punch alone.

The expense of acquiring the quantity of wax which would be needed to fill extremely large cans may justify the extra trouble of the process described in Figures 145, 146, 147. On a core of this kind, the pierced pattern will be more deeply "quilted" than when wax is used.

Fig. 143. "Candernlantels" by Brian Hale. Tin cans pierced with a welding torch for hanging lanterns and hurricane chimneys. Heat from the flame creates different colorations on painted and unpainted cans.

PIERCED CANS

Fig. 144. Without a welding torch, pierced designs can be made by hammering nails into cans. An inner core of wax will support the walls so that they will not be flattened by the pounding operation. (When the contents of the can can be removed through holes, the structure is even stronger.) The impact center punch in the foreground was used to make indentations on the lines of the patterns. As shown on the back row, perforations are then completed with nails.

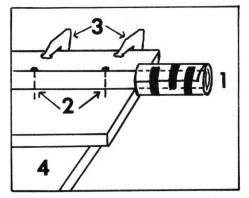

Fig. 145. The core diagrammed here was used for the pierced can in Figure 147. It is constructed by wrapping the end of a 24-inch length of 1-inch doweling with newspaper and taping it securely to make a padded cylinder about an inch smaller in circumference than the can (1). The doweling is attached to a heavy board with screws (2), then clamped or nailed to the edge of a heavy table (3 & 4). The tin cylinder is slipped over the padded extension, and one row of the design at a time is perforated.

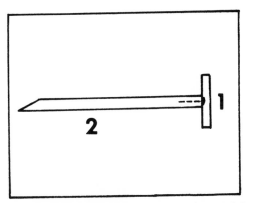

Fig. 146. The pierced chimneys can be used for planter lights by attaching a wooden coaster (1) to a sharpened length of ⅜-inch doweling (2) with a screw. The rim of the coaster will serve as an anchor for the chimney.

Fig. 147. The tin is given a soft antique finish with a torch, and the chimney is set over a vigil candle in a glass cup.

Fig. 148. A slightly different technique is used for piercing the candle warmer in Figure 149. The top is perforated first by supporting the can on a slightly taller can and hammering a nail in the dots of the pattern with just enough force to create dimples. The holes are then pierced with an electric drill. (The dimples are necessary to keep the bit from slipping. They can also be made with the impact center punch.) The large openings around the edge are made with the blade end of a bottle opener.

Fig. 149. The warmer is slipped over the support shown in Figure 145, the pattern on the walls are dented with a nail, and perforated with an electric drill. This method is somewhat faster than that used for the chimney in Figure 147, but it will not produce the same interesting quilted texture.

Salvaging Sheet Tin from Cans

Sheets of metal can be retrieved from cans and used to construct entirely new forms. The top and bottom of the can are removed with a can opener, then the rolled rims are cut off. (Although the rims can be trimmed away with metal shears, a can opener of the type shown in Figure 150 makes the job easier.) The remaining cylinder is opened by cutting out the seam with shears.

To flatten the sheet, it is gradually and gently bent in the direction opposite to its curl. It is then placed on a hard, flat surface and hammered. A pebbled texture is obtained by pounding the tin on both sides with the rounded end of a ball peen hammer.

A jeweler's saw is necessary for cutting out complex motifs which have perforations or acute inside curves, but many patterns can be satisfactorily simplified to adapt them to the limitations of metal shears. The tin is first trimmed close to the outline to remove most of the excess material. Margins around circles and sharp curves should be snipped off every inch or so to keep the shears from becoming bound in the incision.

The walls of cans are too thin for most jewelry unless the tin is used simply as a foundation for designs similar to those in Figure 130. However, it is not too difficult to sweat-solder several layers of metal together to obtain a suitable slab. The laminations must be soldered before the form is cut out. If the design calls for subsequent soldering, the layers should be clamped together so that they will not slide out of alignment when the inner solder is reheated.

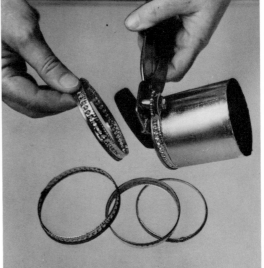

Fig. 150. The top and bottom of the can are removed first, then the rolled rims. With a can opener of this design, rims can be removed intact and set aside for special projects. The cutting wheel is positioned just below the rim, the jaws of the opener are crimped shut to start the cut, and the handle is turned slowly until the circle is completed.

Fig. 151. Perforated rings are obtained when the can opener is positioned so that both the cutting wheel and notched gear are below the rim. Extra pressure is needed to cut through the thick seam.

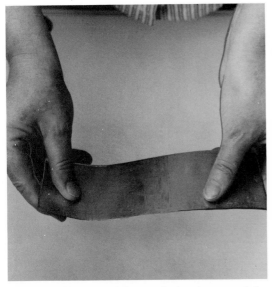

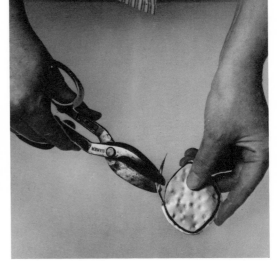

Fig. 152. The remaining cylinder is opened by trimming away the seam with metal shears. Most of the curl is removed by bending it gently in the opposite direction. It is then placed on a hard, flat surface and hammered on both sides until it is flat. The sheet can be textured by pounding it with the rounded end of a ball peen hammer.

Fig. 153. Patterns for tin forms are traced onto the metal and trimmed close to the outline to eliminate excess material. Margins are snipped away every inch or so to keep the shears from becoming bound in the incision.

Fig. 154. Burrs on the edges of cut forms are filed off. The shallow corrugations on some can lids can be hammered flat, though for many projects the pattern is attractive.

Fig. 155. Printed labels and protective inner coatings may be removed from some cans with paint dissolvers, but it is quicker to blister them with a torch and buff away the residue with steel wool. Interesting colors appear when a low flame is played once more over the tin. The lid in front of the untreated can on the left has dark mottlings on a ground of iridescent blue-gray, amber, and turquoise. The lid in front of the partly burned can on the right has subtler tints of blue and lavender.

MAKING TIN FLOWERS

Fig. 156. Circles of two sizes are cut from can lids, textured with a ball peen hammer, and cleaned thoroughly. Unlacquered cans are buffed with steel wool.

Fig. 157. Coatings of paint or lacquer are burned off as described in Figure 155. The circles are divided into equal segments, and the lines are slashed.

Fig. 158. Tips of the petals on the large circle are trimmed, and the segments of the small circle are divided further to make a fine fringe.

Fig. 159. A washer is tinned on the underside, the center of the small circle is tinned on both sides, and the center of the large circle is tinned on the top side. The parts are fluxed, stacked in proper order, and heated until the solder flows between the layers.

Fig. 160. The tip of a length of coat hanger wire is bent at a slight angle to form a stem. The flower head is turned over and the wire is soldered to the center. Leaf shapes can be soldered to the stem or attached to separate wires.

Fig. 161. The flower is shaped by gently curling the petals or turning them at slight angles. The center is made fuller by drawing every other segment of the fringe forward with tweezers before giving each strand a half twist.

Fig. 162. The flower head is sprayed lightly and evenly with opaque enamel and allowed to dry. The center (or edge) is then sprayed from a distance with a harmonious color of enamel to deposit delicate speckles.

Fig. 163. When the paint is dry, a wrapper of thin plastic is taped over the blossom to protect it when the stem and leaves are sprayed.

Fig. 164. The flower has a speckled orange-on-red finish which resembles enameled copper. The stem and leaves are shaded black and green.

Fig. 165. Many other designs can be worked out by making slight changes in the way the circles are slashed and the petals are shaped. For more subtle colorations, the tin can be treated by some of the processes described earlier in the chapter.

Dyeing Cans

As opposed to paints, which are surface colorants, fabric dyes are formulated to penetrate and permanently stain the fibers of woven materials. Since tin cans are nonabsorbent, it would appear incongruous to attempt to change their natural colors by a process intended for porous substances.

Dyes will not affect the appearance of the tin itself, of course, but they will beautifully stain the inner protective linings which are on many cans that are used for foods. Most of the coatings range from shades of pale gold to deep brass, providing brilliant screens to reflect light through the films of transparent color.

The dye bath is mixed according to instructions for fabrics, using a stronger concentration of pigment. Cans or cut shapes are dropped into the simmering dye and agitated gently with a flexible spatula until the color has developed to the desired intensity. (Metal instruments may scratch the coating.) They are then rinsed in clear water and allowed to air dry.

In addition to the use of dyed tin for holiday decorations and household accessories, luminous fragments can be worked into stitchery designs and woven constructions.

Fig. 166. Ornaments from can lids and rings, decorated with gummed seals and bits of self-adhering plastic.

ORNAMENTS FROM LIFT-TOP CAN RINGS

Fig. 167. These opulent baubles are composed of rings from lift-top cans, tiny finishing nails, and stones salvaged from old costume jewelry. They were originally designed to be special gifts for collectors of one-of-a-kind Christmas ornaments. However, if they were set with stones which are less glittery, they could become wearable brooches and pendants.

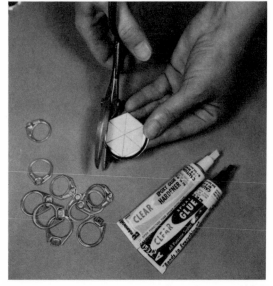

Fig. 168. A pattern is drawn for a base to which the rings will be attached with epoxy glue. The base is cut from a smooth can lid. . . .

Fig. 169. . . . and the points of the rings are buttered liberally with adhesive. They are arranged on the tin form and left undisturbed until the glue has hardened.

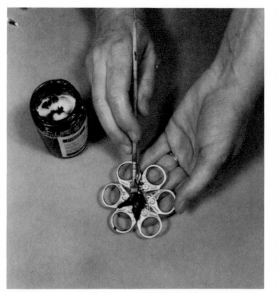

Fig. 170. The metal is antiqued by coating it with black paint and wiping the high spots clean.

Fig. 171. The depressed area between the rings is filled with liquid steel, and the stones are carefully pressed into it. When the steel has set, the ornament is turned over and the process is repeated on the exposed tin on the other side.

chapter 5

Found Wood

Like all materials originating from the growth of living cells, wood is perishable, and earliest examples of wood art disintegrated thousands of years ago. We know that they existed, however, for ironically enough, the craftsman's tools are often more enduring than his products.

Implements for carving wood have been found that date back to the Old Stone Age. Where climates are dry and carved objects have been protected in caves or tombs, wooden sculpture and ornaments of extremely fine quality have survived for more than six thousand years. Many of these ancient pieces exhibit a high degree of professionalism that would be a credit to any artist of the modern world.

TOOLS

Primitive carvings were made with chipped stones, sharp shells, or animal teeth lashed to wooden handles. The vitality of some of the works which were created with these crude implements is evidence that an elaborate workshop might be a rewarding luxury, but it is by no means a necessity. However, with such a bewildering assortment of woodworking equipment to choose from, it is difficult to distinguish between what is essential and what is merely convenient.

Actually, working with found wood is one of the simplest crafts since most of the materials are already preformed. We are not concerned with the special skills and power-driven tools needed for fine cabinet making or complex carving, and many projects require no supplies at all except a sturdy backing and a bottle of glue.

It is better, of course, to have the capabilities for altering the size or shape of wood scraps in order to adapt them to special designs or the limitations of prescribed spaces. A saw and a sharp knife will suffice in many cases, but a collection of some of the multipurpose tools shown in the previous chapter is well worth the cost. A rubber mallet and a few wood chisels are invaluable for more ambitious carvings.

Fig. 172. Wood intarsia doors, by Bob Biancalana, are designed to cover the opening of a storage
compartment. The outline of the basic tree form
was halved, drawn on two sheets of hardboard, and
cut out. The margins were secured to a wood
foundation, and inlays of fragments of weathered
wood were set in with white glue. Touchlatches
eliminated the need for knobs.

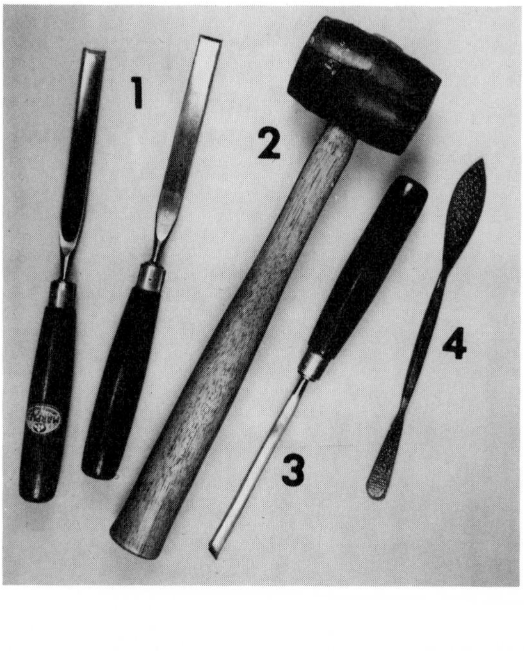

Fig. 173. WOOD-CARVING TOOLS

1. Gouges.
2. Rubber mallet.
3. Skew chisel.
4. Wood rasp.

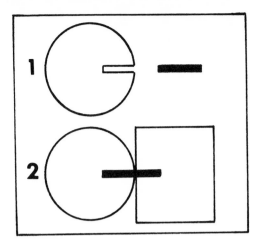

Fig. 174.   MAKING A PEGGED JOINT

1. Holes into which a short length of doweling will fit snugly are drilled at the points of contact between the two wood objects.
2. Glue is dripped into the holes and distributed with a sliver of wood. The dowel is wedged in place to join the objects together.

Fig. 175. "Compartmentalization," by Robert Biancalana, is composed of weathered wood, driftwood, and a few water-worn stones and bones. The battered tin spoon toward the middle of the panel evokes images of an ancient campsite. The pieces are attached to a plywood backing with white glue.

ADHESIVES

There are many reliable wood adhesives in every hardware store. The white glues are acceptable for indoor installations, but epoxy or a waterproof wood glue should be used on compositions which will be exposed to weather. Mosaic assemblages of fragments having irregular contours are best set in a paste-type adhesive, such as tile mastic, or in a ½ to 1 inch thick bed of cement. Magnesite, a fine-grained, slow-setting cement, is a good choice for indoor pieces. It is mixed to a spreading consistency with magnesium chloride instead of water, and may be colored with the same dry mineral pigments used for mortar and concrete.

Where large, free-standing constructions involve a number of wood pieces, glue alone may not be adequate. Nails or screws can be added for extra security and concealed by countersinking the heads and filling the holes with wood putty. Doweled joints are stronger and do not damage the exterior surface.

Fig. 176. "Third Station of the Cross," by Robert Biancalana, is made of pieces of painted and unpainted weathered wood and segments of salvaged construction tiles. Although the scene is portrayed with utmost simplicity, it has a compelling realism. The "throng" in the background appears to be withdrawing uneasily from the harsh, dry road on which a bowed figure lies prone with one arm stretched out lifelessly.

Fig. 177. The basic form for "Sunburst," by Mary Dekker, is a wooden salad bowl. The pattern is built up of scraps of frame moldings and dowels left in their natural colors. (Photo courtesy of the artist.)

Fig. 178. "Hills of Marin," by the author, is perhaps best classed as a mixed-media composition since it is made of marble cubes, red lava rock, and Byzantine glass, as well as assorted fragments of driftwood and scraps salvaged from the workbench of a frame maker. The wood elements predominate, however, and the technique of construction illustrates a method that is appropriate for materials which are not flat.

Fig. 179. It would be difficult and extremely restricting to draw an accurate cartoon on paper for a construction of this kind. It is better to indicate light and dark values and space divisions directly on the framed backing. The materials can then be experimentally arranged until the concept is clarified. Some of the frame scraps are washed with acrylic colors for use where special accents are needed. Carpet tacks are partly hammered into the backing to provide undercuts for the setting bed of colored magnesite.

Fig. 180. Although magnesite sets slowly, it is best to mix only what is needed to work up small sections of the design at the time. Before the cement hardens, edges of the completed area are trimmed close to the decorative materials so that excess cement will not be a problem when new additions are made.

Fig. 181. To make sure that new and old layers of magnesite will bond firmly together, the hardened material should be thoroughly dampened with water and the edges brushed with magnesium chloride before spreading fresh cement in the adjoining area.

Fig. 182. The thick consistency of the setting bed makes it possible to set materials into it at any angle. A three-dimensional effect is achieved in "Hills of Marin" by deeply recessing some elements, leaving others extended outward. Finished magnesite panels should cure slowly out of the sun, preferably covered with a thick layer of newspapers. A liquid waterproofing compound will seal the surface and heighten the color of the decorative inclusions.

TECHNIQUES FOR RESURFACING SALVAGED WOOD

The only rules for working with salvaged wood are those which are arbitrarily established upon individual preferences. They are largely philosophical, rather than technical, and it is probably safe to say that any approach is acceptable—*if it works!*

Some craftsmen consider it a kind of dishonesty to tamper with the natural state of found wood. Others completely reject the restriction of "woodiness," and modify the material in any way that suits their needs, even to the extent of burying it under an encrustation of plaster or paint.

Nothing would be gained by taking an inflexible stand on either of these concepts, for unless the craftsman is content to be repetitive, every new design may require a different approach. The worn paint on the weathered wood in some of Robert Biancalana's intarsias adds a distinct flavor to the work and he has wisely refrained from altering it. (Figures 172, 175, 176.) The strong, rugged character of lumber yard scraps is an equally important element of Stanley Carpenter's mosaic in Figure 183. But in other circumstances, the natural state of these same materials might contribute little more than economy to the effect the craftsman is trying to achieve.

Fig. 183. "Wood Mosaic" by L. Stanley Carpenter. (Photo by Richard Gross, courtesy of California Design, Pasadena Art Museum.)

Fig. 184. Wood construction doors for an art gallery by Mabel Hutchison. (Photo by Richard Gross, courtesy of California Design, Pasadena Art Museum.)

Fig. 185. Processes for altering the surface quality of found wood can range from merely scratching it with a nail to the more involved technique of metal leafing. Lightweight hobby chisels and gouges can be used for carved textures.

Fig. 186. "Instant" textures can be created with hammered imprints of nail heads, screw driver points, the rims of metal lipstick cases, and the like. This is a salvaged redwood block sliced in half diagonally to make bookends.

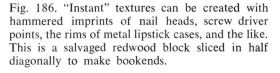

Fig. 187. The textured blocks are rubbed with wood stain and secured to foundation strips of pressed hardboard. Heavy antique brass furnace door hinges are mounted on the corners. A soft green patina on the brass was obtained by the procedure described in Test No. 11, Chapter 4.

Gesso paste has long been used as a painting ground and as a medium for modeling ornate relief designs on frames and decorative plaques. The new pastes, composed of white pigments and special fillers in polymer emulsions, have a number of advantages over the old plaster compounds. They are tougher, more flexible, and stay open for a longer period of time. They are also extremely hard and durable once they are completely cured.

Polymer modeling paste can be applied to almost any kind of material, but it is especially useful for obtaining unique textural effects on objects and compositions where the shapes of the forms are of primary interest, and their identity as wood is of no consequence.

The paste is about the consistency of putty and can be troweled on with a knife or small paddle. Patterns in the wet material can be created with a fork, nail, pointed stick, or a segment of a comb or saw blade. It can also be extruded from cake decorating tubes and flexible catsup and mustard dispensers.[1]

Modeling pastes shrink slightly as they dry and it is best to build up thick reliefs in several layers, allowing each to harden before adding fresh material. Special gels can be mixed with the paste to minimize the formation of small surface cracks which can result from excess shrinkage.

[1] Plunger-type tools designed especially for extruding modeling pastes and plastic metals are available in larger hobby shops. See Index of Supplies.

Fig. 188. Acrylic polymer latex emulsions in paste form can be used to resurface or texture wood and many other materials. This effect was obtained by extruding the paste in vertical lines from a cake decorator. Two layers were applied and when the paste had hardened, sharp peaks were ground off with a file. The form was then gold leafed, antiqued, and wired for a lamp.

Fig. 189. Different eyes evaluate discards in different ways. Sculpture, mosaics, and assemblages can be made from salvaged newels, finials, banister posts, and table legs. Objects of this kind can also serve purely decorative purposes and be made into lamps, oversized candle holders, plant stands, and other functional accessories.

Fig. 190. "Venus," by Art Grant, is carved from a mahogany table leg.

Fig. 191. "Miscellany." Wood construction by Harry Dix. (Photo by
Nathan Rabin, courtesy of Bertha Schaefer Gallery.)

GOLD LEAFING

There are two different kinds of materials which are commonly called "gold leaf." One is made of precious metals, has a karat rating, and is moderately expensive. The other is a simulated leaf (sometimes called Dutch Metal) which is a little brighter in color and about half as costly. Genuine gold leaf is marketed in several forms, each of which has certain features which are advantageous for specialized needs. For the most part, however, the craftsman will find the simulated leaf entirely adequate. Its somewhat glaring brilliance can be readily subdued with stains and antiquing solutions, and when it is carefully finished, it is as durable and beautiful as more expensive products.

Leaf can be applied to clean dry paper, wood, metal, plastic, and glass. (Porous surfaces should be sealed with varnish or gesso.) Clear varnish thinned with turpentine makes an excellent adhesive, though special preparations that dry faster are available.

Leafing is not difficult unless the process is rushed by attempting to apply the leaf before the adhesive has reached the proper state of stickiness. This can create frustrating problems, indeed, for the delicate tissue will tear and crumble and manage to attach itself to fingers, brushes, floor, or any other surface except the one for which it is intended. Experience is the only way to learn how the varnish should feel when it is ready. Perhaps it can best be described as having the dry "tack" of masking tape.

Traditionally, gold leaf was applied over a red-brown undercoating, but it can be equally handsome over almost any rich, dark color, including black. Natural wood tones and pastel tints are not recommended since they are too close in value to the plating to reveal its characteristic weblike fissures.

Where a large area is to be covered, such as the newel post in the following project, only one section at the time should be leafed. The leaf is so thin that overlaps and patches will not be noticeable. The finished plating should be sealed with a coat of clear varnish or spray plastic and allowed to dry before antiquing.

Commercial stains for antiquing painted wood may be used over leaf, or test glazes can be prepared from 2 parts turpentine, 1 part linseed oil, and a small amount of oil color. The mixture is brushed over the leafed object and allowed to dry until it is slightly dulled before the high spots are wiped clean with a soft cloth. If the glaze dries too fast, the amount of turpentine should be reduced. After the glaze is completely dry, it is coated with clear glossy or dull-sheen varnish.

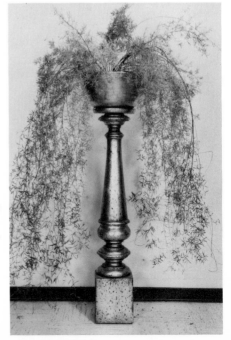

Fig. 192. Large exterior newel posts can be made into lamps, floor candle holders, and plant stands. The wood can be stained, painted, and antiqued, or finished with gold leaf.

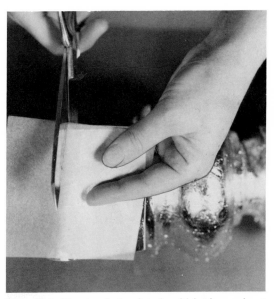

Fig. 193. To prepare the post for leafing, several layers of corroded paint are removed, then the surface is sealed with a thin coat of varnish. On objects of this size, gold leaf adhesive is applied to only one section at a time.

Fig. 194. Sheets of simulated gold leaf are about 5½ inches square and are packaged with tissue paper between the layers to facilitate handling the material. For plating curved surfaces, it is best to cut the sheets into smaller strips.

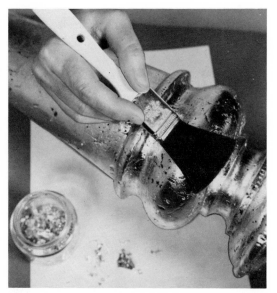

Fig. 195. The adhesive is allowed to dry until it is barely tacky, then one edge of the leaf is pressed against it. The tissue is gently drawn away an inch or so at a time, and the leaf tamped down with a soft clean brush.

Fig. 196. Excess leaf around patches and over-laps should not be removed until the adhesive is dry. It can then be easily brushed off and saved for use on small objects, such as the jewelry in Figs. 199–203. The plating should be sealed with clear varnish before it is antiqued.

TREATMENTS FOR WEATHERED WOOD

Weathered woods have a surface quality that cannot be duplicated by artificial processes. Often, however, some treatment is advisable to remove decayed particles and to protect the wood against further deterioration.

Spongy strata should be scraped away with a knife. Sand, salt, and other encrustations can be removed with a wire brush.

There is no reason why driftwood cannot be colored by any means which produces a desired effect. Penetrating pigments, such as wood stains, will not leave heavy deposits on the surface, nor will oil paints thinned with a mixture of turpentine and linseed oil, nor acrylic paints thinned with water.

Charred driftwood can be very beautiful and colors of amber, brown, and velvety black can be obtained with a propane torch. Charring will also produce fascinating textures on certain kinds of wood since the flame will etch away the softer layers of the grain, revealing in sharp relief the pattern of the hard layers. A great deal of smoke will be created and the work should be done outdoors on an asbestos pad. A pan of water and an old brush should be kept close by so that the smoldering wood can be extinguished at will. Soot and ashes can be removed by vigorously scrubbing the charred pieces with a wire brush.

The natural color of weathered wood can be lightened with commercial wood bleaches or by soaking the fragments in a strong solution of household bleach and water. For a more silvery patina, the wood can be placed in the sun and brushed occasionally with the bleach solution over a period of several weeks.

A shiny finish is seldom appropriate for compositions of weathered wood, but diluted dull-sheen varnish or a thin coat of liquid wax will protect the wood without leaving excessive gloss. Periodic applications of a liquid penetrating sealer are even better, especially for pieces which are to be displayed outdoors.

Fig. 197. A spirited driftwood steed graces the yard of a Mendocino (California) fisherman. His tongue is a worn shoe sole, and his ears are old sandals. Raveled rope serves as a luxuriant mane, and a battered pot protects his head from the weather. He is truly a seaman's horse, as indicated by the rubber boots encasing his hind feet.

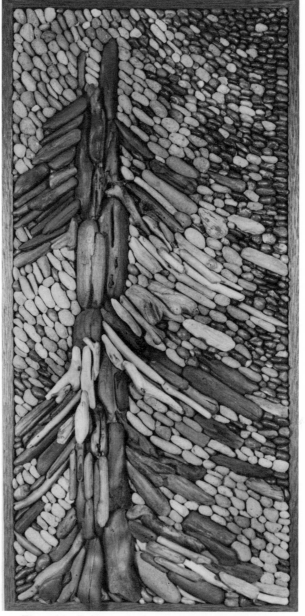

Fig. 198. Driftwood from public beaches has
sometimes been charred in campfires. The fragments in "Tree Bones" range in color from dark
brown to yellow-brown and silvery gray. The
background materials were also collected from a
beach and consist of polished pebbles and bits of
broken bricks worn by the waves into rich terra-
cotta nuggets. The materials were attached to a
wood backing with tile mastic, and the finished
panel was brushed with two thin coats of liquid
penetrating sealer. By Mary Lou Stribling.

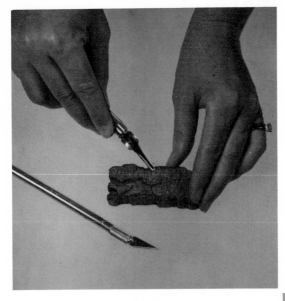

CARVED DRIFTWOOD JEWELRY

Fig. 199. Worn fragments of driftwood often have whorls and striations which suggest forms that can be developed into jewelry. Soft, decayed areas are scraped away first, then some of the etched depressions are gradually carved deeper to define the primary lines of the design.

Fig. 200. Driftwood is usually quite porous, and the completed carving should be sealed with diluted varnish or acrylic medium before finishing it with paint or metal leaf. Silver leaf is applied here only to the highest parts of the relief.

Fig. 201. The entire piece is brushed with a wash of black acrylic paint, and the silver is buffed with a soft cloth while the paint is still wet.

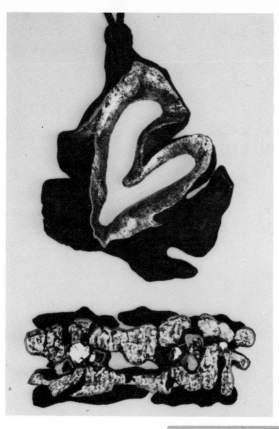

Fig. 202. A few chunks of galena (a lustrous, faceted lead ore) are set in the crevices of the finished brooch, and a pin is secured to the back with epoxy. The pendant above it is stained dark brown and has a lining of antiqued gold leaf.

Fig. 203. The same basic procedure was followed for these examples. The high spots of the pendant have subtle colorations of mossy green and brown that complement the turquoise fragments of Diopase (crystalline silicate of copper) which are tucked into the depressions. The pierced brooch is plated with antiqued gold leaf.

chapter 6

Salvaged Sheet Glass

The story of glass has all the elements of an historical suspense novel—superstition, legend, intrigue, romance. Chapters which were written during the thirteenth to sixteenth centuries, when Venetian glassworkers were exiled on the Island of Murano, even include violence and political corruption.

The fact that the beginning of the story is unrecorded has only served to stimulate fanciful conjectures and scholarly conclusions about its setting and cast of characters. For many years, Pliny's famous tale of the accidental discovery of glass was considered authoritative, but it is now recognized to be a combination of guesswork and earlier folklore.[1]

According to Pliny, a storm forced Phoenician merchants to take refuge on a sandy beach near the mouth of the river Belus. In the preparation of a hot meal, they improvised supports for their cooking pots from blocks of natron (native sodium carbonate) in their ship's cargo. The heat melted the natron, which combined with the sand to form glass.

Although it is naïve to imagine that sufficient heat and other ingredients for glassmaking could have spontaneously been present on this great occasion, one observation is significant. It was evidently known by that time that soda would lower the melting point of sand, and it is one of the glass fluxes still used today.

Glass had been discovered much earlier than the period Pliny described, but most historians agree with him on one point—that it *was* accidental.

But was it? Man has always been capable of original invention and it is not completely illogical to consider that perhaps he learned to make glass from his observations of natural phenomena. There are three kinds of natural

---

[1] The Roman writer, Pliny the Elder (A.D. 23/24–79), is best known for his encyclopedic *Natural History*. The work consists largely of secondhand information, however, and is more valuable for its account of life during this period than for scientific facts.

Fig. 204. "Fire—Still Life" by Ann Hunt. Flattened bottles and salvaged window glass coated on the subsurface with opaque copper enamels.

glass: rock crystal, a pure quartz; fulgurite, a thin, glassy, tubelike formation which on rare occasions is created when lightning strikes sand; and obsidian, which is volcanic glass. It is credible that some ancient people were astute enough to relate the last two happenings to the reaction of sand and rock to great heat. It might have been centuries before this isolated bit of knowledge was combined with more advanced observations to result in a process for making glass, but it is a pattern that is consistent with other inventions of man.

This is an example of fanciful conjecture, of course, for we do not know how glass was discovered, nor where, nor when. Existing evidence places the occurrence in Syria or Egypt over five thousand years ago, so we must at least give Pliny credit for some accuracy about its birthplace.

Glass beads, ornaments, jars, and vases were made first. Transparent glass sheets which could be cut for windows were not developed until much later—probably in Rome about the first century A.D.

Techniques for working with new glass have general application to salvaged glass, but there are a few notable differences. Reliable and tested brands of unused glass can be purchased in whatever quantity is needed to execute a preplanned design. But usable shards retrieved from broken windows and doors, or the trash bins of building wreckers and glass jobbers, will include assorted unknown materials in many irregular shapes and sizes, which means that the design must be adapted to the most practical method of joining such fragments into a single unit. Excluding special techniques for free-standing structures and certain kinds of mobiles, this can be accomplished by *leading, heat-fusing,* or *gluing.*

Leading glass for large windows or screens requires considerable experience as a great deal of weight is involved and the structure must be well supported. Although small leaded projects are entirely within the scope of the amateur craftsman, the subject cannot adequately be handled within the limits of this chapter. But beyond that consideration, leading is not the best answer for joining a large number of small pieces of salvaged glass together. It is tedious for one thing, and the nature of the process dictates a certain rigidity of design.[2] We will investigate the advantages and limitations of heat fusion and adhesives later in the chapter.

[2] Instructions for leading bottle rims are given in Chapter 7. Simple leaded projects are described in *Mosaic Techniques,* by Mary Lou Stribling (New York: Crown Publishers, Inc., 1966), and other titles in the **Appendix.**

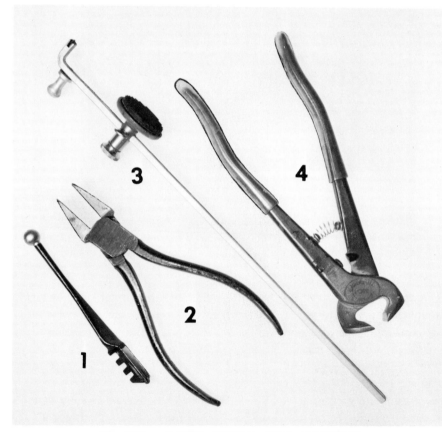

Fig. 205.   BASIC TOOLS FOR CUTTING GLASS
1. Ball end glass cutter.
2. Square jawed glazier's pliers.
3. Glass circle cutter.
4. Mosaic nippers.

CUTTING GLASS

Almost every day of our lives we handle sharp instruments which are potentially dangerous—scissors, knives, needles, ice picks, razor blades, saws—yet cutting glass sounds hazardous to many persons.

Actually, there is small chance of a serious accident as long as a few reasonable precautions are observed. The student may feel more secure wearing lightweight cotton gloves until experience increases his confidence. And it may seem superfluous to mention that it is most unwise to run fingers along a freshly cut edge, or to sweep scraps and splinters of glass from the worktable with bare hands, but a surprising number of beginners are inclined to do so.

Straight Cuts

Although glass can be sawed with special instruments, for ordinary purposes it is *fractured,* rather than cut. To control the direction of the break, it is scored with a glass cutter, then turned over and the thumbs are pressed against the line until it snaps. On thick or textured glass it may be necessary to first start the fracture by tapping along the reverse side of the score with the ball end of the cutter.

The scored line on certain kinds of glass may barely be visible, but with experience, the control required to force the cutter to make the proper "bite" against the glass becomes almost instinctive. Firm, even pressure on the tool should be maintained. Heavy pressure can result in a thick, fuzzy mark which will not break cleanly.

Perfectly straight lines are obtained by using a ruler, T-square, or yardstick as a guide, and if the cut is quite long, the straight edge can be secured to the glass with floral clay to prevent it from slipping. On cuts of this kind, the cutter can either be pushed forward or drawn downward. However, when the lines of a pattern beneath the glass are being scored, it is best to move from bottom to top to keep the hands from obscuring the design. The

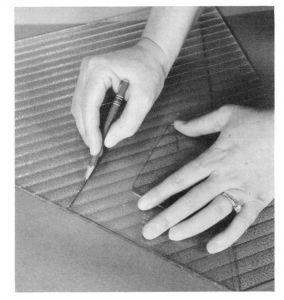

CUTTING STRAIGHT LINES ON GLASS

Fig. 206. The worktable is padded with newspapers or an old blanket to provide a cushion for the glass. Where accurate right angles are desired, cutlines are established with a T-square or triangle and marked with a glass pencil.

Fig. 207. Textured glass is always scored on the smoothest side. For straight cuts, a ruler is secured to the glass with floral clay and used as a guide for the cutter. The wheel is held perpendicular to the glass, and a clean, white line is scratched on the surface.

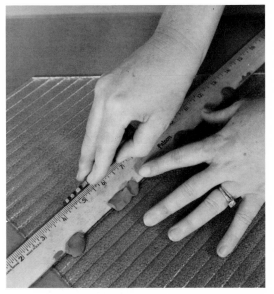

wheel must be kept perpendicular to the glass or the edges of the fracture will be beveled.

Glass should always be cleaned thoroughly before it is scored, for dust and grime will prevent the cutting wheel from making even contact with the surface.

Cutting Circles

The circle cutter shown in Figure 205 is designed along the principles of a compass and will score disks from about 2½ to 24 inches in diameter.[3] The horizontal arm is set to the desired radius and the rubber cap at the axis is pressed against the glass. Floral clay can be wedged against the cap to keep it from sliding when the arm is rotated.

Hands are positioned so that the entire circle can be scored without lifting the cutter from the glass. A few practice swings will reveal where the score should be started. Once the circle is scored, the glass is turned over and pressure is applied to the mark until it is fractured all around.

This form cannot be lifted out as could a hole punched from paper or cookie dough. Several radiating lines must be scored from just outside the circle to the edges of the glass so that when they are fractured, the margins can be removed in sections.[4]

[3] Smaller disks can be obtained with a lens cutter.
[4] Margins around all curved forms are removed in sections as described for circular disks.

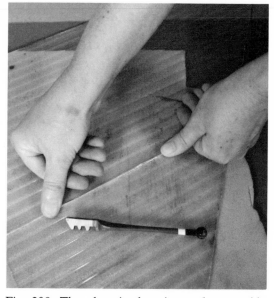

Fig. 208. The glass is then inverted on a thin sheet of foam rubber, and pressure is applied to the score until it snaps. It may be necessary to first start the fracture on thick glass by tapping along the score with the ball end of the cutter.

CUTTING GLASS CIRCLES

Fig. 209. The horizontal arm of the circle cutter is set to the desired radius, and the rubber cap at the axis is pressed against the glass. (Floral clay will help keep it from slipping.) The score is started with the right hand crossed over the left . . .

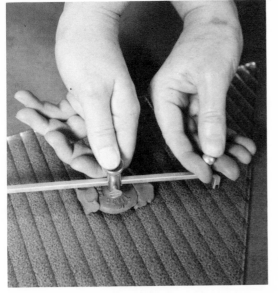

Fig. 210. . . . and ended with the right hand under the left to complete the full 360 degrees without changing the pressure on the cutting wheel. There should be a margin of at least ½ inch between the circle and the edge of the glass sheet.

Fig. 211. The glass is turned over on a padded surface and the circle is fractured by pressing it with the thumbs or tapping it with the ball end of a straight cutter. It is then turned back over, and radiating lines are scored from just outside the circle to the edges of the glass. It is inverted again to fracture the lines and remove the margins in sections.

Cutting Special Shapes

It is possible that there are no shapes which the skilled craftsman cannot cut from glass *if* he has the proper equipment. However, there are many shapes which are difficult to cut by the usual process of scoring and fracturing, and there are some which are best not attempted at all.

It is often more practical to avoid cutting problems than to try to solve them. This can usually be done by making minor changes in the pattern, but sometimes fragmentation or modification of a design would mean completely sacrificing the original concept. In these cases, it is worth taking the time to examine all aspects of the difficulties and then try to work out means of attacking them.

Long, narrow spear shapes are likely to break off at the tips when they are fractured by pressure. If the glass is fairly thin, they can be scored and snapped away with glazier's pliers. They can also be fractured with the strange little tool shown in Figures 212 and 213 which was designed for cutting ceramic tiles. Unfortunately, this instrument is becoming increasingly scarce, but the alternate technique demonstrated in Figures 215 and 216, is perhaps even more versatile.

Its very simplicity is a real innovation, yet it is actually derived from an old method of cutting glass which is still favored by many professional jobbers. It could be called "fracturing from *leverage*." The glass is scored to establish a fracture line, then it is "bent" over a fulcrum which forces the cleavage. Glass jobbers are generally concerned with straight cuts and use a ruler or the edge of a table or board as a fulcrum. But by slipping a wooden match about ¼ inch under the score and pressing the glass downward on each side, clean breaks can be obtained on shapes which might ordinarily be classed as "impossibles."

The method is not recommended for extremely thick or heavily textured glass.

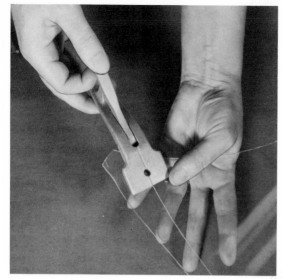

CUTTING SPEAR SHAPES FROM GLASS

Fig. 212. This little instrument was designed for cutting ceramic tiles but it can also be used for certain shapes of glass. It works on a principle of leverage—that is, the glass is scored, then positioned so that the hole in the top of the cutter is directly over the mark.

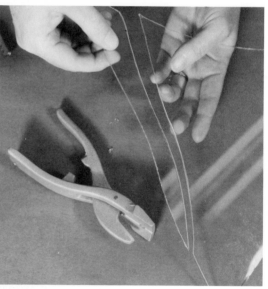

Fig. 213. The under jaw of the cutter is wedge-shaped and serves as a fulcrum over which the glass is "bent" when the handles are pressed together.

Fig. 214. A different leverage technique makes it possible to cut such shapes as the sharp, undulating rays around the sun face on this enameled glass tile. It is also useful for many other kinds of forms where the cutlines are not excessively long.

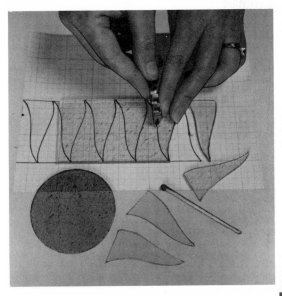

Fig. 215. A pattern for the rays is traced onto a sheet of paper, and a strip of glass is cut as wide as the rays are long. The rays are scored one edge at a time.

Fig. 216. The end of a wooden match is slipped about ¼ inch under the score to serve as a fulcrum. The glass is then pressed down firmly on each side of the match to force cleavage.

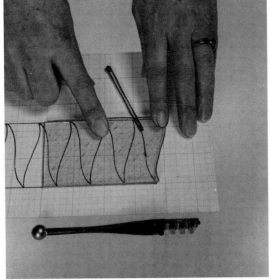

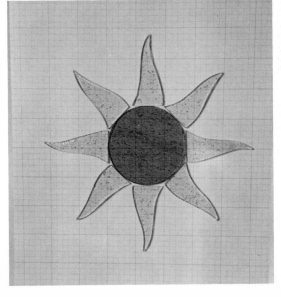

Fig. 217. The parts of the motif can be assembled and glued to a backing, or they can be decorated and kiln-fused to a square of compatible glass.

Forms having inward angles are not impossible to cut from glass, but they do require special techniques. Even though the scored lines stopped precisely at the apexes of the angles, the fractures would continue across the sheet. This would occur on the fish in Figure 218 at the points indicated by arrows.

The very predictability of this characteristic reaction often suggests solutions to the cutting problems it creates. As already mentioned, the best answer is usually to modify the design. Figure 219 shows how two inward angles were eliminated by cutting the head and body separately. The angle of the mouth was rounded into a gentle curve without greatly altering the appearance of the fish.

It would be difficult to use fragmentation as a solution to the cutting problems of the design in Figure 220 without drastically changing its character. The alternate solution demonstrated in Figures 221 to 224 is much more trouble, but it can be used to obtain other shapes with inward angles, such as stars and crosses.

The pattern shown in Figure 220 involves a number of cutting problems, two of which were eliminated by minor changes. The sharp tips on the tail were gently rounded to minimize the chance of having them break off irregularly; the spaces between fins and tail were widened slightly to facilitate removal of glass margins.

To circumvent fractures across the form from the points of the inward angles, small holes were drilled at their apexes to serve as terminals. This is a logical procedure, since a fracture line will not jump over a void unless it is subjected to too much pressure, or unless by accident the cutter slips and scores a mark on the other side.

It is not necessary to invest in expensive power equipment to drill holes in glass. Drills designed for metal or wood are not suitable, of course, but glass bits which fit an ordinary "egg beater" hand drill can be obtained from manufacturers of glass tools. Sometimes, used bits can be purchased from jobbers who install doors and windows.

To start the hole, the glass is placed over a sheet of thin foam rubber (or a scrap of carpeting), and the bit is seated firmly at the spot where a hole is desired and twirled rapidly and lightly until a slight depression is created. When white glass powder forms around the bit, the friction must be reduced by lubrication or the drag of metal against glass can cause a fracture. The bit should be dipped into turpentine or light oil from time to time when resistance is felt.

After the glass is penetrated by the tip of the bit, it is turned over and the hole is enlarged to the proper circumference from the other side.

Once holes are drilled at the apexes of inward angles, the form is scored, fractured, and margins around it are removed in sections. Few shapes will require the elaborate method of breaking excess glass into the small pieces shown in Figure 222, but all should be studied to determine which margin to remove first. Numbers on the pattern for the enameled fish indicate the order which was followed.

CUTTING GLASS FORMS WITH INWARD ANGLES

Fig. 218. Designs of this kind which have inward angles can be broken down or modified to eliminate the probability of fractures at the points indicated by arrows.

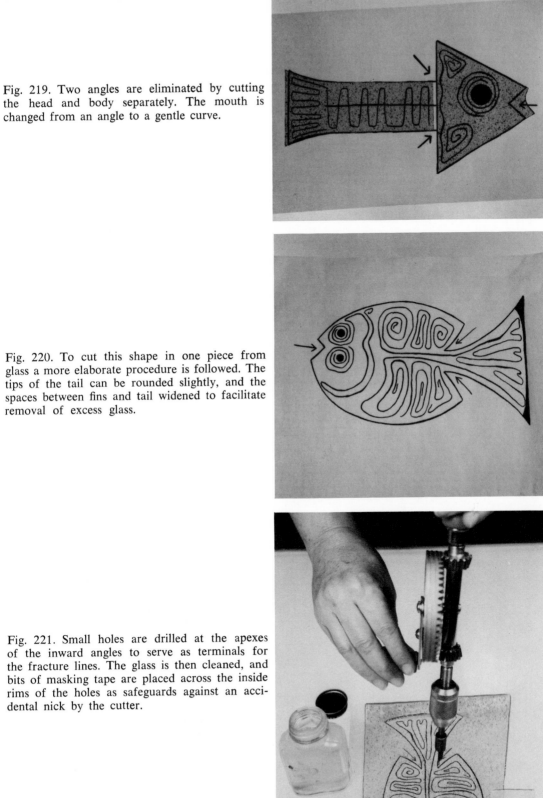

Fig. 219. Two angles are eliminated by cutting the head and body separately. The mouth is changed from an angle to a gentle curve.

Fig. 220. To cut this shape in one piece from glass a more elaborate procedure is followed. The tips of the tail can be rounded slightly, and the spaces between fins and tail widened to facilitate removal of excess glass.

Fig. 221. Small holes are drilled at the apexes of the inward angles to serve as terminals for the fracture lines. The glass is then cleaned, and bits of masking tape are placed across the inside rims of the holes as safeguards against an accidental nick by the cutter.

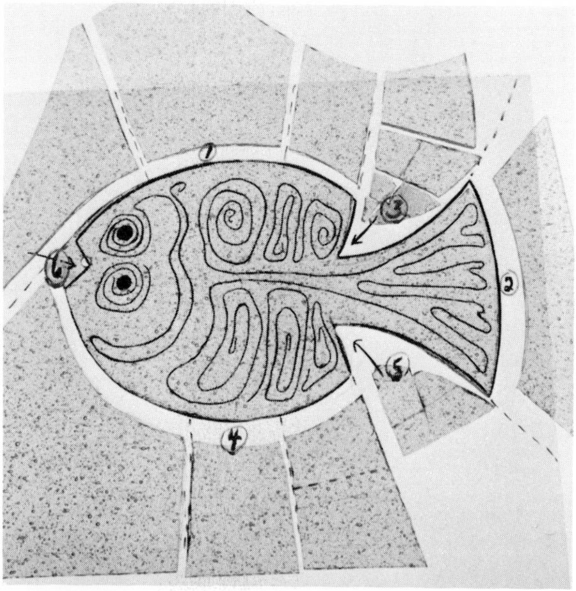

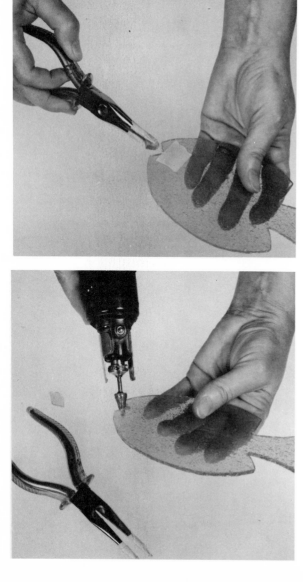

Fig. 222. The outline of the fish is scored and fractured, then the margins are removed in sections. The numbers on the pattern indicate the order that was followed here.

Fig. 223. The small bits of glass in the inward angles are removed last. Long-nosed pliers padded with a layer or two of masking tape can be used to gently work them out one at a time.

Fig. 224. The edges of the cut form are refined with a small emery-tipped electric drill.

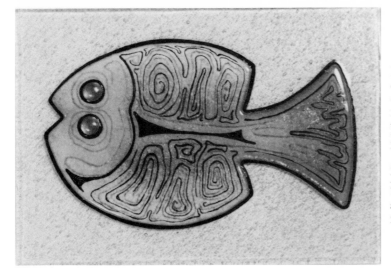

Fig. 225. Red, yellow, and orange opaque copper enamels were sifted onto the glass fish and sgraffitoed with a toothpick. The enamels were kiln-fired, then accents of black ceramic overglaze were added on top. The form was kiln-fused to a rectangle of bubbled cathedral glass. (Enameled glass is discussed more fully later in the chapter.)

KILN-FIRED GLASS

Most studio kilns for firing glass and clay are heated by gas or electricity, but in the past twenty-five years, electric kilns have become increasingly favored because of their price, safety, convenience, and portability. They are also manufactured in a variety of styles and sizes, ranging from miniatures, which are handy for tests and jewelry, to giant models which can accommodate large sculptures or a great quantity of ceramic pieces.

Kilns are designed for either low-fire materials, such as glass and earthenware, or for high-fire materials, such as stoneware and porcelain. Since the difference in cost between the two is relatively small, a high-fire kiln is a more practical investment for persons who desire to fully explore the ceramic world.[5]

Some kilns have a lid and others are loaded from the front. Economy models may be turned on by the simple act of plugging them in, while certain deluxe models have graduated heat controls similar to those on kitchen ovens. Kilns can be equipped with cutoffs which automatically terminate the firing when the desired temperature has been reached or with pyrometers which register the interior temperature at all times.

Features of this kind should be weighed against special goals and budget limitations. Interior space, for example, may be more important than convenient refinements. Once a selection is made, the operational instructions should be studied carefully and a trial firing made with the kiln empty. Several additional firings of tests and pieces of insignificant value should be made before firing something which represents a great deal of time.

Clay and glass are both ceramic materials

[5] Nearly all high-fire kilns of moderate size require a 220 V. electrical outlet.

Fig. 226. Small economy-model kilns lack the convenient features of deluxe models, but they can enable the craftsman with a modest budget to experience the excitement of working with ceramic materials. This is a top-loading kiln with the lid removed. The arrows indicate a pyrometric cone positioned where it can be observed through the peephole. Glass scraps to be melted into rounded nuggets are arranged on the shelf. Although most economy kilns have metal stands, it's a good idea to place them on a board covered with sheet asbestos.

but there are vast differences in how they must be handled and designed, and in how they react to heat. Heat is used to change clay from a plastic substance to a permanently hard, durable product. Heat is used to change glass from a rigid state to a temporarily flexible state during which it can be reshaped before it is cooled and rehardened.

To accomplish these things successfully, it is necessary to understand the natures of clay and glass. A fully comprehensive treatment of these subjects is beyond the scope of this book and suggestions for further study are listed in the Appendix.[6]

Since the firing techniques for all ceramic materials have certain basic relationships, suggestions for firing clay as well as glass are included in the following notes.[7]

Notes on Firing Clay and Glass

• A coating of kiln wash should be applied to the floor of the kiln and the top sides of shelves to facilitate removal of glaze drippings or scattered fragments of glass.

• A separator must always be used between glass and the surface on which it is fired. Dry whiting or powdered asbestos will serve for this purpose, though commercial glass separators are more convenient and reliable. Most of these products are applied to kiln shelves and molds like whitewash, and need not be reapplied until they become scarred or chipped.

• Glass must be clean before it is fired. Fingerprints and dust can be removed with household glass cleaners. If the glass has been stored in areas where it might accumulate a residue of hard, greasy materials, it is best to remove the film with denatured alcohol, then wash the glass in hot, soapy water, rinse it thoroughly, and polish it dry.

• All ceramic ware should be completely dry before it is placed in the kiln, and during the early stages of firing, the kiln lid should be propped open about an inch to permit steam and other fumes to escape.

• Glass and clay should be heated slowly to prevent fractures from trapped steam or

[6] Detailed instructions for working with clay and glass are given in *Mosaic Techniques,* by Mary Lou Stribling (New York: Crown Publishers, Inc., 1966).

[7] Clay projects are discussed in Chapter 10.

from the shock of abrupt temperature changes. Once they are thoroughly heat-soaked, firing can proceed rapidly.

• There should be a space of at least an inch between kiln elements and objects being fired. Even more space should be left around large glass plates, bowls, tiles and thick hand-molded clay forms.

• It is risky to fire glazed and raw clay pieces together. If the raw form should explode, bits of clay may settle on the glazed ware and become permanently attached.

• The temperature required for fused glass projects will be different for different kinds of glass, and may vary according to the rate of heat rise and the way the kiln is stacked. The range is usually between 1350° and 1500° F.

• Pyrometric cones are used to determine when specific kiln temperatures have been reached. There is enough leeway on the maturing points of most clays so that no harm is done if they are fired a little lower or higher than the temperature considered perfect. Glass firing is much more critical and a few degrees often makes a great deal of difference. A cone serves primarily as a warning that a critical stage is approaching. The kiln lid is then slightly lifted periodically to watch the progress of the glass. The firing is not terminated according to a precise temperature, but rather according to how the glass looks. Most kilns have certain spots which are hotter than others, so that if the kiln is fully loaded, important pieces should be placed where they can be observed.

• Pieces of glass which are heat-fused together must be *compatible* or they will fracture. This means that they must expand and contract at the same rate. Compatibility cannot be determined by color, texture, or thickness of the material, so preliminary tests of scrap glass should always be fired before they are combined in a finished project.

• Different clay bodies are formulated to mature at different temperatures. When these temperatures are reached, the kiln is turned off and allowed to cool before it is opened. However, when glass has reached the desired state of viscosity and the heat is turned off, the kiln lid should be propped open slightly for about a minute to allow latent heat to escape. Otherwise, the glass will continue to melt further, sometimes to a point where the piece is ruined.

• Thick glass laminations are more likely to crack than thin laminations. The danger can be reduced by annealing, which prevents the temperature from dropping too rapidly, thereby insuring a more even saturation of heat. To anneal glass in a kiln equipped with a pyrometer, the heat is turned off when the desired viscosity has been reached, and the door is propped open about an inch until the pyrometer has dropped down to 1250°–1300° F. The door is closed and heat switched on low for fifteen minutes, then turned off. Lacking a pyrometer, the elements can be allowed to cool down to a dull red color before turning the heat back on for the final soaking cycle.

Fig. 227. The propane torch which was used for soldering metal and charring wood in previous chapters will get hot enough to melt glass rods, tubes, and small fragments of soft glass. To hold it in a horizontal position so that the glass can be freely manipulated in the flame, a supporting rack can be made from heavy wire or a metal towel rack. An asbestos pad should be placed beneath it.

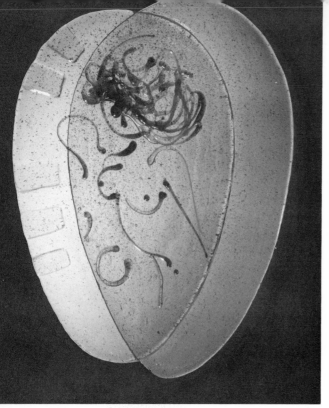

Fig. 228. This bouffant nude might be called a glass sketch. Scraps of cathedral glass were twirled in the flame of a propane torch until they were molten, then threads were pulled out with long tweezers and snapped off. Two overlapping glass blanks were positioned on a mold; the threads were arranged on top and temporarily secured with rubber cement. After kiln-firing to 1375° F, the glass had assumed the shape of the mold, and all parts were smoothly fused together.

TECHNIQUES FOR DECORATIVE FUSED PROJECTS

As mentioned in the notes on firing glass, compatibility is an important factor in the success of kiln-fused projects, for if two pieces of glass do not expand and contract at the same ratio, they will fracture apart during the cooling cycle or at some time afterward. Salvaged glass which is very old or has been exposed to weather for an extended period may have tiny fissures which can cause it to split when it is cut or fired. It may also have encrustations on the surface so minute that they may be invisible to the eye, yet once they are fired, they become an unpleasant scummy skin.

A thin coat of clear glass glaze will circumvent the problem in most cases, and will not change the color of the glass itself. Colored glass glazes over colored glass can be used for subtle tonal variations as long as the base glass is not too dark.[8]

[8] Prepared glass glazes can be purchased from ceramic supply houses and craft shops. See Index of Supplies.

Glass tiles are good choices for experimenting with decorative techniques as small scraps can be utilized and the individual units can be planned as parts of larger compositions. The tiles shown in this chapter can be made from flattened panes of bottle glass as well as from salvaged stained glass.

Enameled Glass Tiles

Many enamels manufactured for decorating metals may be fused to glass. Transparent enamels can be used to tint colorless glass to a limited degree, but when they are applied heavily enough to create deep shades, they will usually craze. They are most effective when laminated between two layers of glass, where they will form delicately colored bubbles.

Certain colors of opaque enamels are less stable than others, but most will bond beautifully to soft and medium-hard glass. Fairly accurate judgment as to the hardness or softness of glass can be made by firing an assortment of cathedral, bottle, plate, and window glass chips of approximately the same sizes to 1450° F. The edges of soft glass will be completely rounded; some may even be melted into half-spheres. Domestic bottle and window glass will be less round, and the edges of plate glass may barely be blunted.

Opaque enamels lose much of their brilliancy over a transparent foundation. To keep the colors from being weak and spotty, a reflective screen of liquid gold overglaze was applied beneath the enameled motifs in Figures 214, 225, 235. Silver or platinum overglazes would also serve for this purpose.

The inward angles between the rays of the moon symbol in the following project were eliminated by separating the rays from the central circle. They can be cut out one at a time from small scraps. However, if a piece of glass 6½ to 7 inches square is available, the entire motif can be cut more accurately by the double circle method shown in Figures 229 to 235. The chips removed from between the rays are uniform and can be saved for other geometrical designs.

The number of rays around the circle is optional up to a point. Too many slices of a fairly small circle would create terminal angles so acute that they would be difficult to score and fracture.

A pattern for the moon face was drawn on lightweight typing paper, then it was cut carefully along the outline of the profile and the curve representing the shadow of the earth. The face itself was discarded and the remaining two pieces used as stencils.

Gum solution, which is used for holding enamel granules in place before they are fired, will secure the stencils to the glass. A second application of gum on top of the paper will minimize buckling and prevent scattered enamels from falling onto the glass when the stencils are removed.

A fine-mesh sifter is needed for applying the enamels. The 80-mesh sifter in Figure 233 has been covered with four layers of nylon stocking material secured with a rubber band.[9]

[9] By using a sheet of clean paper under the glass, scattered siftings of enamels can be returned to their containers. If it is impractical to handle the glass between siftings of more than one color, mixed enamels can be collected and stored in a scrap container. When a usable amount of material has accumulated, it can be tested for color. Sometimes subtle blends are produced which cannot be purchased commercially.

MAKING AN ENAMELED GLASS TILE

Fig. 229. A cutting pattern for the motif is drawn with a compass and ruler. For eight rays, the circle is divided into sixteen equal parts.

Fig. 230. A circle cutter is secured to the glass with floral clay, and two concentric circles are scored. The inner circle is scored first, then leaving the cutter attached, its arm is extended and the radius is reset to equal the distance from the center to the tips of the rays. After the second circle is scored, the margins are removed as described earlier in the chapter.

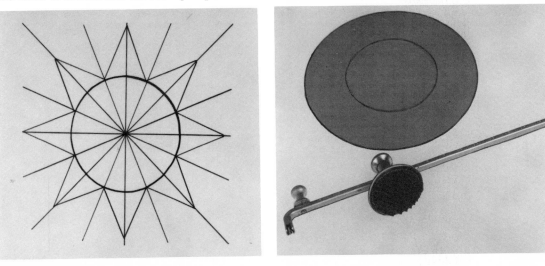

Fig. 231. The form is placed over the pattern, and the inner circle is freed by scoring and fracturing the lines between the rays. This divides the outer frame into eight equal parts, from which the rays are separated one at a time. The photograph shows the parts in place with one ray completed. A second ray has been scored and reversed, and is being fractured with the ball end of a straight cutter.

Fig. 232. The basic form is coated with ceramic gold overglaze, and fired gold-side-up on a prepared kiln shelf to 1200° F, or until all the black fumes have burned away.

Fig. 233. The glass circle is placed gold-side-down on a sheet of clean paper and brushed with gum solution. Stencils for the moon face are pressed in place, and the entire circle is recoated with gum. Lemon-yellow enamel is sifted over the glass, making the application heaviest along the profile, then the central stencil is peeled away.

Fig. 234. Pale green enamel is sifted along the inner edge of the remaining stencil. After it is removed, the green enamel is dusted lightly around the entire circumference of the glass circle. "Doodle" patterns are scratched on the face with a toothpick before the gum dries. On another sheet of paper, the rays are arranged in a row, coated with gum, and sifted with lemon-yellow enamel, shading into canary yellow at the tips.

Fig. 235. A base square of glass is centered over the pattern and the parts of the motif are arranged on it, using dabs of rubber cement for temporary security. The slab is fired on a prepared kiln shelf until the enamels are smooth and the edges of the glass are rounded. Temperatures will vary according to the glass used. This example was fired to 1375° F and annealed.

Bubbled Laminations from Ribbed Glass

The current popularity of glass craft has led to an increasing scarcity of real bargains in salvaged stained glass, but happily, precious materials are not a prerequisite for creativity. Ordinary window glass can be changed to something quite extraordinary by treating the subsurface with drifts of pigments and gold leaf.[10] If a kiln is available, a lifetime can be spent working with the common uncolored discards from a glass jobber's bench, for they can be sagged into molds, flashed with glass glazes, painted with low-fire glass colors, plated with metallic overglazes, or colored with copper enamels. Fused laminations are even more exciting, though space permits but a glimpse of the many facets of the subject.

Bubbles in fused glass laminations are produced when air or other gases are trapped between the layers. Sometimes this is an acci-

dental occurrence, and sometimes bubbles are deliberately created by inclusions of glass glazes, enamels, or mica flakes. Bubbles produced by these materials are not totally predictable as far as their size and spacing are concerned. But sections of ribbed window glass can be arranged with the textured sides facing each other so that air enclosed in the depressed areas will form characteristic bubble patterns. With experimentation, they can be predetermined with considerable accuracy. When the ribs are placed at right angles, round bubbles in precise rows will be formed. Diagonal crossings will create long, pointed bubbles, and sometimes teardrops.

Semiobscure ribbed glass is used for windows, doors, and shower stalls. Scrap products should be identified by a glass jobber or by firing a series of tests, for not only are domestic and imported brands incompatible, but each has unique reactions to heat.[11]

[10] This process is described later in the chapter.

[11] See Index of Supplies.

Domestic ribbed glass fires to crystal clarity and is compatible with many brands of untextured domestic window glass. A product called "Pluralite" was used for the following projects. The imported ribbed glass used is a Belgian product which is sold under several different brand names. It must be pretreated to prevent the formation of a surface scum, but it is a fascinating material to work with. Both glasses are available with ribs of different spacings. The Pluralite experiments were made from material $\frac{3}{16}$-inch thick with ribs $\frac{3}{8}$-inch apart. The ribs of the imported glass were $\frac{1}{2}$-inch apart.

Multiple laminations usually require more heat than two layers, and should always be annealed. If the ribbed sandwiches are fired too low, the air pockets will be flat and ragged instead of smoothly domed and glistening. The thick pieces shown in Figures 236 to 238 were fired between 1525° and 1550° F. However, temperature notations should be used as guides, not rules, for allowance must be made for variances in pyrometers, kilns, and firing conditions.

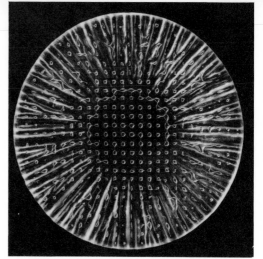

Fig. 237. Two matching Pluralite circles were arranged with the ribs facing and crossing at right angles, then they were sagged into a textured plate mold. On the sloping sides, the bubbles are deformed and sometimes connected. When similar laminations are fired on an untextured shelf or plain shallow mold, the bubbles are round and precisely spaced like those in the bottom of the plate.

Fig. 236. Three squares of Pluralite, a domestic ribbed glass, were used for this paperweight. Their edges were painted with black glass color, and the two matching bottom blanks were stacked with sides aligned and smooth sides facing. The smaller square were positioned on top with ribbed side down. By arranging the ridges to cross on a bias, oblique bubbles were formed.

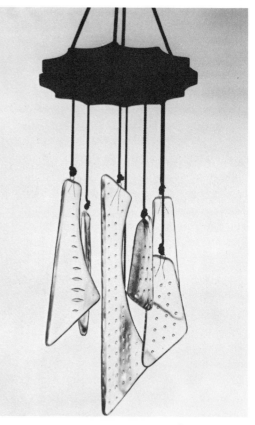

Fig. 238. Experiments with random arrangements of scraps of ribbed glass will produce a variety of bubble patterns. These chimes were made from margins left over from cutting the glass circles for the bubbled plate. Nichrome wire was fused between the layers for suspending the pieces.

Frosted Patterns in Glass

The most common causes of scum on the surface of fired glass are improper cleaning and overfiring, but sometimes it stems from the composition of the glass itself. Some products can be melted almost to a state of total fluidity and remain beautifully transparent. Others will stay clear only to a certain temperature, and thereafter become increasingly opaque.

Such tendencies are usually regarded as a nuisance, but they have a direct relation to the satiny, translucent patterns which appear to float inside the slabs in Figures 240 and 241.

The imported ribbed glass does not form ordinary bubbles in the spaces defined by the intersecting ribs. Instead, the walls of the pockets become frosted, and assume varying shapes according to the way the rib lines cross.

Rows of squares are formed when the ribs are arranged facing and intersecting at right angles. Diamond-shaped patterns result from cutting one or both blanks on a bias. With a little experience, the placement of the frosted spots can be anticipated, making it possible to stagger them in multiple layers as shown in Figure 241. To prevent the surface from becoming frosty and semiobscure, it can be coated with glass glaze or glass flux before firing. Surprisingly enough, luster will also prevent scum.

Fig. 239. Matching squares of Belgian ribbed glass are cut so that the ribs cross on a bias. The smoothest side of the upper blank is coated thinly with colorless glass glaze, and the smoothest side of the lower blank is painted with unfluxed black glass color. The squares are stacked with ribbed sides facing. . . .

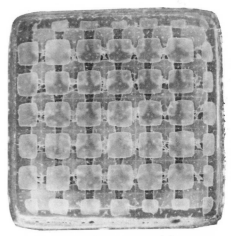

Fig. 241. This paperweight was made from four squares of Belgian ribbed glass arranged in pairs with ribs facing and crossing at right angles to make a grid. One sandwich was stacked on the other, and the exposed surface of the top blank was coated with colorless glass glaze. The block was fired to 1500°–1550° F.

Fig. 240. . . . and fired on a kiln shelf coated with glass separator. Between 1500° F and 1550° F the slab is perfectly fused, and the frosted pockets between the ribs are slightly elevated. For bookends, slabs of this kind can be epoxied to L-shaped metal or wooden supports.

Iridescent Patterns

Lustered glass can be a bit overwhelming, and as evidenced by some of the cheap glass which flooded the market a few years ago, it can also be remarkably ugly. But the bowl in Figure 243 has a muted iridescence and a delicate pattern which is quite unlike the usual lustered products.

Lusters are applied to glass in the same manner that they are applied to glazed clay, though on clear glass, the pale lusters (such as mother-of-pearl and opal) are not effective. Fugitive colors will not survive the temperatures required to soften glass, but orange, rose, cranberry, and purple lusters contain gold and within a range of 1450°–1500° F. will change to varying shades of pink with golden overtones.

The luster should be brushed on quickly and evenly, using a fairly full brush. Puddles or droplets can be smoothed by lightly patting the wet luster with a ball of cotton wrapped in a piece of silk.

Ordinarily, when overglazes of any kind are fired between layers of glass, the sheets must be prefired to burn away the oils in the medium. Otherwise, the dark smoke would be trapped inside the fused slab. This precaution is unnecessary for projects like the lustered bowl since the intersecting ridges separate the sheets long enough to allow the fumes to escape before outlets are sealed.

Scalloped shapes are more difficult to cut from thick textured glass than circles or straight-sided figures, and it is advisable for the beginner to start with simpler forms.

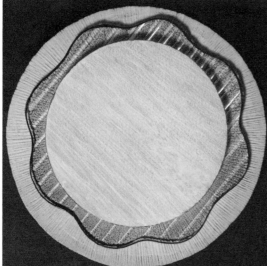

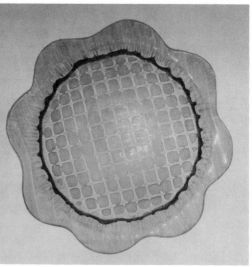

Fig. 242. Following a pattern drawn to fit a simple terra-cotta bowl mold, two blanks are cut from Belgian ribbed glass. The ribbed side of the scalloped form is coated with purple luster, the smoothest side of the central circle is brushed thinly with colorless glass glaze, and the mold is coated with glass separator. When all materials are dry, the glass forms are stacked on the mold with ribbed sides facing and ridges crossing at right angles.

Fig. 243. The kiln is vented until luster fumes have burned away, then the lid is closed. The firing is terminated when the glass has sagged into the mold and its edges are rounded. The finished bowl is a soft pink with golden overtones. The laminated area has a delicate pattern of iridescent squares.

Translucent Colored Bubbles

China paints are low-fire materials which are not usually associated with fused glass projects because the paints mature in the range of cones 020–018 (1202°–1328° F), which is lower than the temperature required to soften glass. Some of the colors, however, will withstand more heat and will produce translucent bubbles in laminations of ribbed glass. Dark colors are apt to appear spotty, but yellow, apple green, light blue, aqua, and the like have sufficient translucence to be appropriate.

Both of the ribbed glasses described earlier can be used and a comprehensive series of tests will clarify the process. The tests can be made from scraps; however, the two kinds of glass cannot be combined for they are incompatible. Observations should be directed toward three areas: thickness of the application of paint, arrangements of the rib lines, and the firing temperatures which produce the best results.

Dry or moist china paints are thinned with painting medium to make a fluid paste, and the mixture is ground on a glazed tile or saucer until it is perfectly smooth. After brushing it on the ribbed side of the glass, it can be patted into an even film with a cotton ball wrapped in silk.

Effects are more luminous if only one blank in a lamination is colored. By cleaning the paint from the ridges with a smooth stick or a piece of silk wrapped around the finger, additional light will be transmitted through the fused piece.

Although laminations of domestic or imported ribbed glass will be fused in the range of 1475°–1500° F, the colored bubbles are more dramatic at a little higher temperature. The test slabs in Figures 244 to 246 are illustrative.

As in the preceding projects, the angles of the intersecting ridges will determine the shapes of the bubble formations. In addition, the character of the bubbles will vary according to which blank is coated. If the upper blank is painted, clear bubbles will appear to float above a film of color. If the placement is reversed, the bubbles will be pearly and semiopaque.

TEST SLABS FOR COLORED BUBBLES

Fig. 244. Thinned china paint is brushed on the ribbed side of a scrap of glass, then the application is pounced lightly with a cotton ball wrapped in a piece of silk.

Fig. 245. Several pieces are prepared to test different colors and thicknesses of paints, including samples on which the ridges are wiped clean with a soft wooden stick or brush handle.

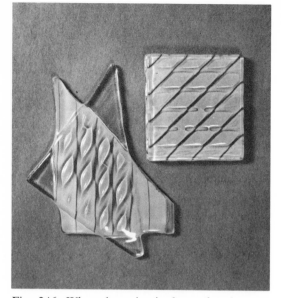

Fig. 246. When the paint is dry, colored scraps are stacked with clear scraps, ribbed sides facing. Some are arranged with the colored layer on top, and some with the clear layer on top. After firing to 1500° F, the bubbles were not fully developed in the test on the right. The test on the left was fired 50° higher.

Making a Segmented Form

Laminated forms involving a number of pieces of glass should be designed so that seams between segments in the upper and lower layers are staggered. In the foundation layer of the yellow moth in Figure 250, the wings are not segmented, but are cut to fit against the body as shown in Figure 248. The upper layers of the wings overlap the body and reinforce the structure.

The pattern is drawn on tracing paper so that lines are visible on both sides.

The body is cut in one piece and an extra head is cut slightly larger than the pattern so that a loop of nichrome wire can be laminated between the antennae. Textured glass is always cut on the smoothest side. Small parts are most easily cut by scoring one edge of the outline at a time and snapping away the margins with glazier's pliers.

The mobile demonstrated in Figures 247 to 250 is made from Pluralite. If Belgian glass is used, the exposed glass surface should be brushed with colorless glass glaze.

MAKING A SEGMENTED FORM

Fig. 247. The wing foundations are cut first along the outside edges of the pattern, then the pattern is turned over and the segments of the top layers are cut along the inner lines. Care is taken to arrange the glass so that rib lines will be alike on both sides. Antennae, body, and extra head are cut from small scraps.

Fig. 248. The glass is cleaned and the under wings are replaced over the pattern with smoother sides up. Margins are painted with black glass color; the smoother sides of the body and antennae are painted solid black. The *ribbed* sides of the segments which form the top layer of the wings are coated with lemon-yellow china paint, and the ridges are wiped clean.

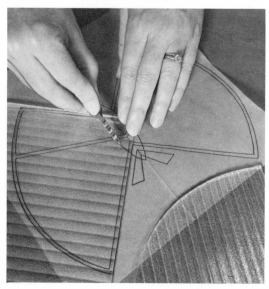

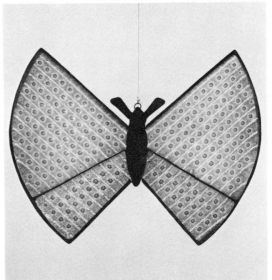

Fig. 249. The body is positioned in the center of a prepared kiln shelf, painted side down, and the under wings are fitted against it with ribbed sides *up*. Upper segments are placed on top with ribbed sides *down*. Antennae are arranged next with a wire loop between them. The head is set in place last.

Fig. 250. The laminated form is fired to 1500°— 1550°F, annealed, and cooled slowly. An interesting translucent pattern of bubbles and lines developed in this example. The china paint appears to be slightly crinkled and drawn around each bubble, giving the wings a texture that resembles dimity or dotted Swiss fabric.

GLASS DESIGNS ON TRANSPARENT BACKINGS

In glass designs which are secured to backings with adhesives, all kinds of scrap products can be combined without regard for size or chemical make-up, which are important considerations in fused projects. They can also be mixed with assorted oddments which could neither be fired nor leaded.[12]

Flat transparent fragments can be attached to window glass, plate glass, or heavy sheets of plastic with a clear epoxy adhesive. Irregular chunks will be more secure in little individual "cushions" of a clear marine sealer which remains flexible enough to adapt to temperature changes without pulling away from the backing. These products are commonly used to calk boat windows and to seal leaks around

plumbing joints, and are available in hobby shops and hardware stores.[13]

Epoxy is packaged in two components: the resin and the catalyst, or hardener. Different ratios of catalyst to resin are required for different brands. (Directions are noted on the labels.) Some of the new epoxies set up quickly and it is best to mix only small amounts at a time in a foil-lined jar lid. Finished compositions should be allowed to cure about a week in the sun or a warm location before hanging them.

A transparent panel can be installed over an existing window by setting strips of wood molding against the panel and tacking them to the window frame. By supporting the panel on spacers, it can be elevated above a wooden backing so that light can pass through and around it.

[12] See Chapter 9, Mixed Media.

[13] See Index of Supplies.

The multi-layered design in Figure 251 is epoxied to a sheet of double-strength window glass. A pattern was drawn for the base layer of colored glass rectangles and the individual sections were cut out. The pattern was then taped to the underside of the foundation as a guide for gluing the glass segments in place. After twenty-four hours, holes were drilled through the panel to mount it above a wood slab as shown in Figure 252. One-inch square clear plastic boxes were used for spacers.

By mounting the panel at this stage of development, bolt-heads and spacers were concealed when other elements of the design were glued on top of them.

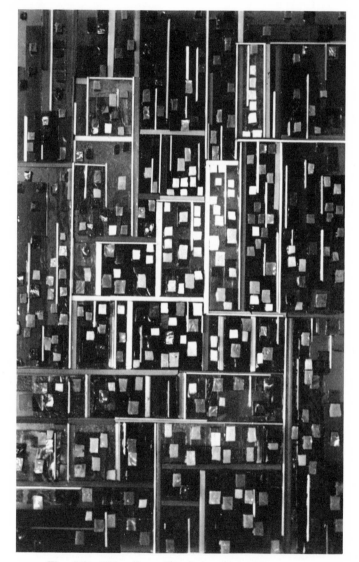

Fig. 251. "The Late City," by the author, is a multi-layered glass mosaic epoxied to a foundation of double-strength window glass. The base layer of the design was cut from scraps of blue, green, turquoise, and amber stained glass. Strips of opaque ribbon glass were arranged over the seams, and small squares and rectangles of colored glass were superimposed to suggest distant buildings and darkened windows. Brilliant blocks of opaque Byzantine glass complete the composition.

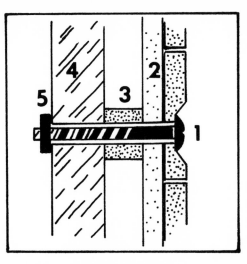

Fig. 252. Transparent panels can be mounted out from wood slabs on spools, plastic boxes, corks, square wooden beads, and so on, with various elements of the pattern arranged to conceal bolt-heads and spacers. If the panel measures less than 15 inches square, four bolts set in about 2 inches from the corners will be sufficient, provided several epoxied spacers are also used.

Holes are drilled through the glass panel, and the top edges are beveled so that bolt-heads will be flush with the surface. The panel is positioned on the slab, and spots for matching holes are marked and drilled. The bolts (1) are threaded through the panel (2), spacers (3), and slab (4) and secured with a nut (5) on the back side.

GLASS DESIGNS ON OPAQUE BACKINGS

When transparent glass is placed over an opaque surface, light rays cannot pass through it and must instead be bounced back from a reflective undercoating of some kind. A coat of white paint on the backing will provide excellent reflection if it is not obscured by a colored adhesive. The white glues and transparent epoxies are suitable for panels which are composed of fairly small pieces of glass. However, plywood and pressed hardboard backings are seldom absolutely level, and even tiny protuberances can keep large sections of glass from making adequate contact. A cushion-type adhesive is indicated for designs of this kind, either tile mastic or a setting bed of cement as demonstrated in Chapter 5.

Most white mastics remain fairly flexible but have good bonding qualities as long as crevices between the attachments are filled with grout. The tile mastics in more general use are yellowish or brown, and the subsurface of the glass must be opacified to screen them out.

Metal leaf is one answer to this problem, as is a kiln-fired undercoat of metallic ceramic overglaze which was used under the enameled motifs discussed earlier in the chapter. Beautiful effects can be obtained with both of these materials, though they greatly alter the character and color of transparent glass.

Copper enamels can be fused to glass, then the pieces set in adhesive with the enameled side *down*. There are tremendous possibilities in this technique, since a single color of enamel will produce a wide range of shades under different colors of glass. In addition, the surface of the glass which rests on the kiln shelf can be textured by applying the glass separator in various ways. The tiny pocks and craters on the glass in Ann Hunt's panels were created by firing the sections on sand. They add an ancient, eroded quality to the materials, which is further dramatized by rubbing dark grout into the pits.

Grout can be mixed with water alone, but white glue or special cement additives will reduce shrinkage and porosity. For dark grout, a wetting solution is made of one part white glue to three parts water. One part black mortar color is blended with eight to ten parts dry grout. (Other cement colors may be substituted, and one to two parts vermiculite, perlite, or sand can be added for texture if the spaces in between glass sections are not too narrow.) The fluid solution is stirred into the dry ingredients a little at a time to make a paste about the consistency of pancake batter, then it is spread over the panel and forced into the crevices with a flexible plastic or rubber spatula. The glass is cleaned lightly with paper towels, and when the grout has set, it is polished with damp sponges and rags. If cracks or pin holes develop, a thin mixture of fresh grout is rubbed into them.

Figs. 253, 254. "Flower in Earth" and "Fire" by Ann Hunt.

Ann Hunt's glass compositions are made from flattened bottles, salvaged window glass, and assorted scraps of stained glass. The individual sections are cut out, turned over, and coated with opaque copper enamels. They are fired on a prepared kiln shelf which has been sifted heavily with sand to texture the glass. The designs are reassembled on plywood or pressed hardboard backings and secured with tile mastic. Black grout, mixed with a small proportion of sand, is rubbed into the crevices between the glass segments. When excess grout is cleaned from the surface, tiny deposits remain in the depressions and subdue the brilliance of the colors to a rich glow. (Photos by permission of The Storm Center.)

COLORING GLASS WITHOUT A KILN

Transparent glass lacquers dry quickly and it is difficult to obtain an even coverage on large areas. They are most suitable for fragmented designs, and are more interesting on textured glass than on smooth glass.

Although the colors will fade from continued exposure to bright sunlight, they are durable enough for seasonal decorations, such as the candle arrangement in Figure 255.

Combinations of colored varnishes and metallic leaf on glass offer opportunites for truly imaginative exploration, for no two pieces will ever be exactly the same. Either smooth or textured glass can be used for the following experiments, though in most cases, the color patterns are exciting enough in themselves without the added element of texture.

The color films described in experiments Nos. 5 and 7 can also be applied to the top surface of mirror fragments, since the mirror will replace the reflective subsurface provided by the leaf. If the mirror is used in a design for a functional surface, such as a box lid or table top, it should be covered with a protective sheet of clear glass or plastic.

Instructions for applying gold leaf are given in Chapter 5 and are not repeated here. The process is the same except that sealer coats are not necessary.

1. Varnish is darkened with burnt umber, burnt sienna, or black oil paints, and brushed onto the glass. (A light fluid varnish is best. Heavy-bodied varnishes should be thinned with turpentine.) When it has begun to set up, another coat is applied to the glass, using a circular motion to create an irregular swirled pattern. Gold leaf is applied when the varnish has dried to the proper tackiness.

2. Varnish is colored with oil paint and brushed onto the glass. (Any color may be used, with the exception of those which are too pale to be effective.) Without waiting for it to dry, a sheet of leaf is carefully dropped over it and gently pushed with the fingers here and there to cause it to split and form interesting crinkled patches. When the varnish is completely dry, the leaf is smoothed with a soft brush and coated with clear varnish. A second unbroken layer of leaf is laid when the varnish is tacky.

3. Varnish is tinted with a cool color of oil paint and brushed unevenly on the glass. Scraps and dustings of salvaged gold leaf are scattered over it. When the varnish is dry, it is sprayed lightly with clear varnish or a pale, transparent color of paint. A layer of silver leaf is applied immediately and smoothed with a soft brush after the adhesive has set.

4. Two matching pieces of glass are cut and sharp edges are removed with an electric grinder or carborundum paper. One piece of glass is painted fairly heavily with thinned oil paint and the other is placed on top to make a sandwich. The two pieces are forced apart, using the point of a knife blade if necessary to break the suction. When the paint is completely dry, it is coated with clear varnish and plated with gold, silver, or iridescent leaf.

5. A wide, flat pan is half filled with water and a small amount of black enamel is dribbled on the surface from a toothpick. A few drops of a contrasting color of enamel are added and the toothpick is dragged through the film to set it in motion. A piece of glass is lowered flat into the water, lifted out and set at an upright slant to dry. Leaf is applied over the marbleized color.

6. Delicate cloudlike veils can be added to the marbleized pattern in technique No. 5 by using two separate dips. The first is made as described and allowed to dry. In another pan of water, several drops of white enamel thinned slightly with turpentine are dribbled over the surface. The water is agitated and the glass is dipped. Leaf is applied after it is dry.

7. A thin wash of turpentine and brown oil paint is mixed. Varnish is brushed onto the glass and spattered with the thinned paint. Scribbles and doodles of opaque colored

Fig. 255. A grove of glass trees was made from scraps of textured glass cut into elongated triangles and coated on the textured sides with transparent glass lacquers. ¼-inch wood dowels were cut into lengths from 12 to 24 inches. The ends were sharpened, and one side of each trunk was flattened slightly on coarse sandpaper. The dowels were painted green, then the flat sides were glued to the glass with epoxy. Trees and candle cups were secured in a block of styrofoam. The base was concealed with fresh greens. (Photo courtesy of CHRISTMAS IDEAS, 1964. © Meredith Corporation, 1964. All rights reserved.)

enamels are immediately trailed into the wet
coating with a toothpick. (The pigments will
separate and spread into feathery patterns.)
Leaf is applied after it is dry.

Fig. 256. Marbleized patterns on
scraps of mirrors, created by the
techniques described in Experiments No. 5 (left) and No. 7
(right).

Fig. 257. A rectangle of window glass was cut
to fit the recessed area of the box lid, and the
underside was treated with brown, scarlet, and
black paints as described in Experiment No. 7.
Gold leaf was applied when the color film was dry.
The glass was glued in place, and thin strips of
balsa were glued on top to conceal the edges.

chapter 7

Bottles and Plastic Discards

Bottles have a certain mysterious quality which evades identification, yet people have responded to it in various ways throughout the history of bottlemaking. The quality is not necessarily related to beauty. Perhaps it has some association with the classic shape of a bottle—a swollen cavity with a narrow neck which is intended to "contain" something. The contents can be as benign as perfume or rare wine, or as malevolent as poison, but often, long after they are gone, the bottle seems to retain some elusive aura.

In an attempt to personify this aura, ancient storytellers inhabited special bottles with capricious genies and demons. Even today in certain rural areas of the southern United States, "voodoo" trees, made by impaling bottles on the tips of the branches, can be found in old cemeteries and near the entryways to houses. Some of the old people profess to believe that the colored light inside the curving glass arches is irresistibly attractive to

haunts and evil spirits. Once inside the bottle, the unwelcome beings can never again find the narrow exits to their glittering prisons.

The earliest Egyptian bottles were produced by laboriously winding molten threads around a sand core and they were understandably reserved for the nobility. About 300 B.C. Syrian glassworkers invented the blowpipe, making it possible to blow a bubble of glass inside a mold. From the time of that momentous discovery, the art of bottlemaking progressed rapidly and spread throughout the civilized world.[1]

The same basic process is used today to make commercial bottles, though measured amounts of liquid glass are mechanically blown and pressed into molds. With the elaborate equipment in modern glass factories, bottles are manufactured in such vast quantities that it is not surprising that they are discarded in

[1] Freely blown forms which did not utilize molds were not produced until about the first century B.C.

145

proportionate numbers.

But perhaps we are too insensitive about those throwaways. One has but to examine the price tags on old bottles to realize how inevitably "today's junk becomes tomorrow's heirlooms." It is possible that within another decade or so, glass bottles will be almost obsolete, for even now, liquid materials are being increasingly marketed in plastic and metal containers.

Economical production is one reason, and another is even more obvious—*glass breaks.* As far as the life of a container is concerned, a broken bottle is the end of the story. But in the story of salvaged art materials, it is only the beginning.

Fig. 259. "Voodoo" trees are still assembled in isolated rural areas as traps for evil spirits. Bottles are impaled on the branches for years until often, the tree ceases to grow and becomes a skeleton of glass-capped spines. This grove of magic trees shows an astonishing selectivity. All the bottles are blue. But since the "old folk" who collected them have died, no one knows whether the choice derived from a color preference, or from a belief that some benevolent aura from the original medicinal contents remained in the bottles.

Fig. 258. "Pop" bottle, encased in a fabric collage. Clear matte acrylic medium was used as an adhesive and to waterproof the decoration. The stopper is a wooden cabinet knob glued to a cork.

Fig. 260. The weathered opacity of driftwood contrasts pleasantly with the crisp transparency of glass on decorative compositions. The flower clusters and leaves on this panel were made by breaking bottles and scrap glass into random fragments and picking out shapes of various sizes which resembled leaves. Small chips and crumbs were used for blossoms. The glass was rounded in a kiln and attached to the driftwood and backing with epoxy.

BAS-RELIEFS FROM BROKEN BOTTLES

Large bas-reliefs can be made from broken bottles if the pattern is designed so that it can be cut into sections which will fit on a kiln shelf. The sections are fired separately, then reassembled on a backing and secured with clear epoxy.

The heavy pressed-board backing for the panel in Figure 264 was painted with blends of flat colors, shading from warm grey at the top and bottom into cool off-white near the center. The board was cross braced on the back side to insure complete rigidity.

Hundreds of leaves in many sizes were cut

or nipped from flattened fragments of clear, green, and brown bottles. Some of the light green and colorless leaves were brushed with liquid gold overglaze, then coated with a ceramic marbleizing solution to cause the plating to separate into delicate veining. A small number of amber-yellow and orange leaves were cut from scraps of cathedral glass.

A quantity of leaves in each color was fired separately, but many were fused into clumps by stacking them as shown in Figures 262 and 263. (Cathedral glass cannot be fused with bottle glass. The two materials are incompatible.)

A pattern was drawn for the trunk and branches, then cut at logical junctures into fireable sizes. The patterns were transferred onto prepared kiln shelves with carbon. The shelf was covered with thin plastic wrap to keep dustings of the separator from becoming intermingled with the glass fragments while they were being arranged. (Plastic wrap will burn away without leaving a deposit on the glass.)

The trunk was built up by placing small chips of unflattened glass along the outline, then filling in the middle. Small crumbs and chips were arranged close together and piled up in several layers, using rubber cement to keep them from sliding. Slabs of firebrick coated with glass separator were set against the seams as "retaining walls" so that the segments would fit back together again after firing.

The trunk sections were fired twice. The first firing was only high enough to fuse the pieces together and allow the stacked chips of glass to sag into the open spaces beneath them. Leaving the firebrick slabs in place, pockets and thin spots were stacked with additional glass and the segments were fired until they had rounded into cobbled forms.

Undersides of the trunk and branches were liberally buttered with epoxy and attached to the panel, then the fused leaf clumps were placed. Extra leaves were layered on top as needed to conceal seams and fill in the composition.

GLASS BAS-RELIEFS

Fig. 261. Hundreds of leaves in various sizes and colors are cut from flattened fragments of broken bottles. A simple pattern is used for large leaves, but smaller leaves are nibbled into freer shapes with tile nippers.

Fig. 262. Some of the leaves are stacked in overlapping clumps and fused together. Others are fired separately. Small branches and twigs are formed by lining up short lengths of unflattened bottle glass on the pattern lines, then placing an overlapping layer on top. Strips of fire brick are set against the joints of the segments so that they can be fitted together after firing.

Fig. 263. The leaves are fired until the edges are rounded but the shapes are still distinct. Large leaves on the right were cut by a pattern. Those on the left are "happenstances" and scraps trimmed with tile nippers. The veined leaves at the top are coated with marbleized gold.

CUTTING BOTTLES

Special equipment is required for slicing bottles with ·complete accuracy and where there is need for only one or two perfect forms, it may be best to seek the services of a lapidary or professional glass worker. An abrasive tungsten carbide rod which fits a hacksaw frame can be used to cut bottles, but the process is so laborious that it might be justified only if the bottle is rare, or too large to cut by other methods.[2]

[2] See Fig. 123.

Bottles can also be cut (or rather *fractured*) by thermal shock and though a special instrument is required, it can be constructed by any inventive "gadgeteer" with an understanding of electricity.[3]

The principle behind cutting glass by this method is the same that causes a hot glass to break when it is placed on a cold surface. Glass expands as it heats and contracts as it

[3] A construction diagram and complete instructions for building a hot-wire bottle slicer can be found in *Mosaic Techniques*, by Mary Lou Stribling (New York: Crown Publishers, Inc., 1966).

RED MADONNA. By Mary Lou Stribling. Yarn remnants of assorted weights and fibers attached to a hardboard backing with white glue.

GARDEN FENCE. By Mary Lou Stribling. Dyed seeds and whole spices attached to a pressed hardboard backing with white glue. Reprinted from FAMILY CIRCLE magazine. (*Photographed by George K. Nordhausen. © The Family Circle, Inc., 1969.*)

SEA GARDEN. By Mary Lou Stribling. Nails, thin brass rods, washers, staples, and tin disks secured to slabs of driftwood.

BIRD OF THE ANGEL SPHERE. By Nick Nickolds. Collage-montage of magazine papers. (*Photograph courtesy of the artist.*)

ESTRELLA DE LA NOCHE #8. By Robert McChesney. Animal bones colored with acrylic paints, sisal fibers, and found metal forms set in opaque polyester resin. (*Photograph by Joyce Brooke.*)

PLOWED FIELD. By Ann Hunt. Salvaged glass colored on the subsurface with opaque copper enamels. (*Photograph courtesy of the artist.*)

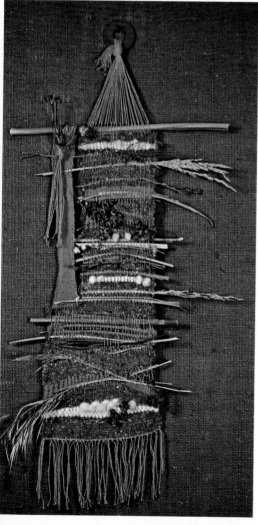

PRIMITIVE WEAVE hanging by Joan Sestak. Handspun wool yarns, seeds, and dried grasses.

PLANT IMPRESSIONS in clay. By Mary Lou Stribling.

Fig. 264. The fired glass is as-sembled on a pressed hardboard backing and attached with clear epoxy. The trunk and branches are olive green. The foliage is dark green at the top of the panel, shad-ing downward into emerald. Chartreuse is introduced near the upper center. Marbleized gold amber, and pale green leaves trail down the trunk, becoming brown, yellow-amber, copper, and brilliant orange on the single twig growing upward from the lower left.

Fig. 265. "Wisteria" is a similar composition, epoxied to Plexiglass and mounted out on spacers from a framed panel as described for "The Late City" in the preceding chapter. Colorless bottles, coated with gray glass glaze on the second firing, are used for large sections of the vine. Other branches and leaves are made from brown bottles. Blossom clusters are scraps of mauve cathedral glass and melted bottle nuggets coated with rose glass glaze.

cools. If extreme temperature changes are abrupt, the internal stresses which are created can cause the glass to fracture.

For cutting bottles, there must be some means of restricting these stresses to a predetermined line so that the direction of the break can be controlled. Figure 266 shows a "bottle slicer" which is designed to cause glass to expand and contract suddenly along the path of an electrically heated nichrome wire. To guide the fracture, the bottle is first weakened by scoring a line around it with a glass cutter. It is then placed inside the nichrome loop and the heat is turned on. When the wire is red-hot, the heat is turned off and within a few seconds the bottle will fracture on the scored line.

In connection with this technique for slicing bottles, I would like to point out the inade-quacies of another theory which is persistently believed by many persons who have not actually tried to put it into practice. The theory is that a bottle can be cut by tying a kerosene-soaked string around it, setting it afire, and plunging the bottle into cold water when the kerosene has burned away.

It sounds logical enough, and the glass will certainly fracture. However, even if the glass has been scored, the breaks will follow random paths which usually include vertical cracks. This happens because the heat is not intense enough and is not concentrated in a narrow line. The flames rising from the burning kerosene not only heat the string, but a fairly wide area of glass around it as well. With an abrupt change of temperature, the glass is likely to crack in several different directions.

CUTTING BOTTLES BY HAND

Fig. 267. A cutline is marked around the bottle with a glass pencil or felt-tipped pen, then a strip of masking tape is placed slightly to the side of the line to serve as a guide for the cutter. The bottle is seated on a piece of thin foam rubber, and the line is scored while rolling the bottle slowly forward so that the cutter moves away from the body.

Fig. 266. This device for slicing bottles was made from two salvaged transformers providing 6 to 10 volts each at 10 amperes, 19–20 gauge nichrome wire, a toggle switch, line cord and plug, 2-terminal soldering lug, and miscellaneous wire and hardware. An aluminum breadpan was used as a chassis. A cutline is marked on the bottle, edged with masking tape, and the line is scored with a glass cutter. The slicer is elevated on bricks or boards so that the nichrome loop is level with the scored mark, the bottle is placed inside the loop, and the heat is turned on. The bottle is turned slowly so that it is heated all around, then the heat is turned off. If the fracture is not complete, the bottle is turned and the procedure is repeated. It may be necessary to fracture thick bottles by dripping cold water on the heated line.

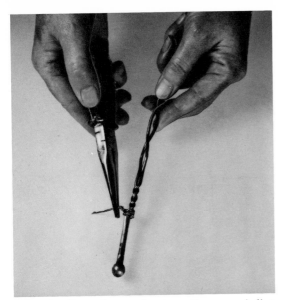

Fig. 268. In order to fracture the scored line from *inside* the bottle, the ball end of a worn cutter is sawed off and attached to a twisted coat hanger with wire. It can be further secured with blobs of solder or by wrapping it tightly with tape.

The simplest way to cut bottles without special equipment is demonstrated in Figures 267 to 270. The broken edges will not be completely smooth, but sharp tips and ledges can be refined with an emery-tipped drill. Emery cloth on an electric oscillating or belt sander will do an efficient job of polishing the rims, though it takes a little time. It is important to remember that a kerchief or mask should always be worn when grinding glass.

For making vases, cannisters, candle holders, and hanging lights from cut bottles, the edges can be coated with plastic metals or bound with self-adhering lead tape or U-channel lead came.

The hand method can also be used to slice rings from bottles. Irregularities are of no consequence if the rings are to be used for mobiles, since they can be rounded by heat. It is best to score the entire bottle before fracturing the separate rings apart. If they are fractured one at a time, the cut edge should be bound with masking tape as a precaution against injury when subsequent rings are scored.

Fig. 269. The coat hanger handle is then bent slightly so that when it is inserted through the neck of the bottle, the ball can be tapped around the scored mark.

Fig. 270. Once the score has fractured, cleavage is completed by gently twisting the two sections apart, or by striking the *outside* of the fractured line with a wooden spoon or stick.

Fig. 271. For her tinkling mobile of free-form rings, Dorothy Saunders cut green bottles into irregular slices from ½ to 1-inch wide and fired them in a kiln until they became rounded. Dry glass separator was sifted on top of the kiln shelves to add an interesting texture to the subsurface of the glass. Refired bottle glass is extremely hard and the rings give off clear, bell-like tones when they strike against each other.

Fig. 272. Fired bottle bottoms make beautifully convoluted disks for mobiles, translucent mosaics, or container lids. For thick medallions, several bottoms can be fused together as long as the glass is compatible. The circular folds of the medallions will drape in different ways according to whether the bases or the cut edges of the bottoms rest on the kiln shelf.

Fig. 273. The melted bottoms are handsome companions for rings in wind chimes and mobiles. To use them for lids, a disk of clear glass is cut to fit inside the mouth of the container and is epoxied to a fired medallion to form a lip.

Fig. 274. Covered containers can be made from all kinds of trimmed bottles and used to store soap, candy, dried foods, and other household items.

LEADING THE RIMS OF CUT BOTTLES

Cames (or *calms*) are grooved strips of lead used in the assembly of glass designs. H-channel came is inserted between two glass panes or the sections of stained glass windows to join them together. U-channel came is used to bind exposed edges of glass. It is an excellent material for professionally finishing the cut rims of medium to large bottles. The material is too bulky to shape readily into small circles.

At first glance, the metal will appear to be hopelessly kinked and twisted, but it will become straight when it is properly stretched. This can be accomplished by stepping on one end of a strip, grasping the other with pliers and drawing it upward until it will no longer give. (A vise can also be used to anchor one end of the came.) It is important that the lead be fully stretched or the binding will loosen after a period of time.

The lead is soft enough to be cut with a sharp penknife, though a scroll saw will penetrate the metal more gently without flattening the walls of the channel.

There are several ways to mold the binding smoothly around the bottle rim. The method demonstrated in Figures 275 to 279 is one of the easiest, but a bit of practice may be necessary to get the feel of handling the lead.

Lead has a very low melting point and tests should be made on scraps to determine how much heat can be used for soldering the seam. If the joint is liberally fluxed, solder can be dripped into it from the tip of the iron and polished smooth with a file.

To keep the finished binding from rattling or slipping, crevices between the glass and came are packed with glazing compound. Commercial products can be used for this purpose, or the following mixture can be prepared: 2 tablespoons whiting, 2 tablespoons plaster of Paris, 1 tablespoon turpentine, 1 tablespoon linseed oil, 1 teaspoon black mortar color. If the mixture is too thick to force into the crevices, it can be thinned with a few drops of turpentine. After about twenty-four hours, the glass is scrubbed clean with dry whiting or fine steel wool.

LEADING BOTTLE RIMS

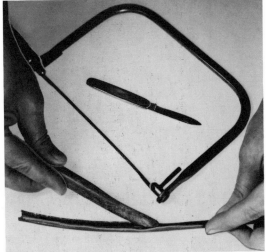

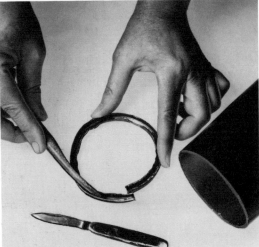

Fig. 275. A length of stretched U-channel lead came is cut slightly longer than the outer circumference of the bottle. The channel is widened with a smooth wooden modeling tool and one end is trimmed at a slight angle to compensate for the smaller measurement of the inside of the bottle.

Fig. 276. The came is shaped gently into a circlet of approximately the size needed, taking care that it does not become twisted. Folds in the inner wall of the channel are reopened.

Fig. 277. Starting with the freshly cut end, the came is seated around the rim of the bottle, using tape if necessary to hold it in place. Excess lead is trimmed away so that ends meet exactly without overlapping. Ripples in the soft metal are "ironed" out with the wooden tool. From time to time, the bottle is turned upside down on a cushion of newspapers, and the neck is tapped firmly with a rubber mallet or hammer to flatten the top of the binding.

Fig. 278. When the binding fits snugly against the glass, the seam is soldered and smoothed by running the iron lightly across it several times. The joint is then polished level with a file and steel wool.

Fig. 279. The inside of the came is ironed once more, then the bottle is set leaded side down on newspapers to finish molding the outside of the binding. Glazing compound is rubbed into the crevices between glass and binding. After 24 hours, the glass is scrubbed clean with dry whiting or fine steel wool.

Fig. 280. A simple base for the finished torch can be made by drilling a hole in a block of wood to accommodate the neck. These examples are joined to old stoneware bottles by long corks wedged inside the necks, and are trimmed with twisted fiber cording.

Fig. 281. Many ordinary objects can be combined with bottle chimneys to make unusual candle lights. Here, the neck and bottom have been cut from the same kind of bottle shown in the preceding demonstrations. A wooden salt shaker is epoxied inside the foot of a plastic bowl to form a stand.

Fig. 282. The top of the shaker is spread with epoxy, the bottle neck is wedged over it, and the candle cup is epoxied in place inside the chimney. The rim of the torch and the seams on the stand are covered with several layers of plastic metal, allowing a drying period in between each. The hardened metal is burnished with the back of an old spoon.

Fig. 283. The bottom and top sections can be removed from tall bottles to make colored chimneys for candles. The rims can be finished by the methods just described, or they can be ground smooth with an electric sander and emery cloth. A coarse grit abrasive is used first, graduating to medium grit, and finally fine grit.

UNCUT BOTTLES

Bottles having interesting shapes but nondescript colors can be upgraded into decanters and vases with paper or fabric collage designs. Clear matte acrylic medium is the best choice for an adhesive, and by applying several coats of the medium over the finished form, the bottle can be washed without damaging the collage.

The bottle in Figure 258 is decorated with motifs cut from a porous cotton fabric. (Slick finishes and tight weaves are not as absorbent and are more difficult to shape against the bottle.) Acrylic medium was brushed on the bottle, the fragment was smoothed into it, then medium was brushed on top of the fabric until it was saturated. Other pieces were added, fitting them together like a mosaic. Patterns for small areas were made by placing a sheet of tracing paper over them, drawing the outline, then cutting out the shape from fabric. When the bottle was covered, the seams were outlined with acrylic paint. A wooden cabinet knob was glued to a cork and painted the same color. Acrylic medium was brushed over the bottle and stopper and after it was dry, both pieces were antiqued. Four additional coats of medium were applied, allowing a drying period in between each, to waterproof the decanter and give it the sheen of polished leather.

Paper collages can be attached to bottles the same way. Being less flexible than fabric, however, paper fragments must be quite small on the necks and sharply curved areas of the basic forms.

Uncut bottles can also be heat-sagged into molds to make bowls, dishes, and ash trays. In most cases, the glass is remarkably improved in quality when it is refired, and often resembles fine crystal.

The compartmented dish by Kay Kinney in Figure 284 is an excellent example of this technique. Two Italian chianti bottles were filled with water and drained. Gold-colored flakes of phlogopite (a bronzy-colored mined

mica) were sprinkled into the wet bottles and distributed with a stiff wire. Bits of colored crushed glass were added and arranged in the same manner. The bottles were fired on a mold until they had fused smoothly together.

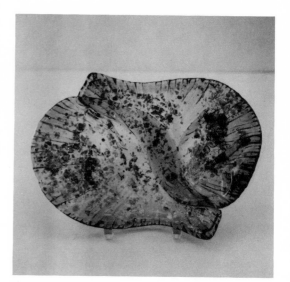

Fig. 284. Compartmented dish from wine bottles, by Kay Kinney. The bottles were placed side by side on a terra-cotta mold with necks pointing in opposite directions and were fired until the glass had sagged into the mold. The overlap of the bottles forms a slight dividing ridge. The texture and modeling of the mold are imprinted on the subsurface of the dish. (Photo courtesy of the artist.)

Fig. 286. This prim lady is evidently attired for a meeting of her garden club or flower-arranging class. The metal cap of a green bottle was wrapped with olive-green raffia and epoxied in a depression on the underside of an iron coaster. Bands of plastic metal were added on each side of the raffia trim to conceal the cap and strengthen the attachment. Melted glass nuggets were epoxied on for eyes, and black cord was glued on to define the features. The plant container is a can, painted black and wrapped with raffia.

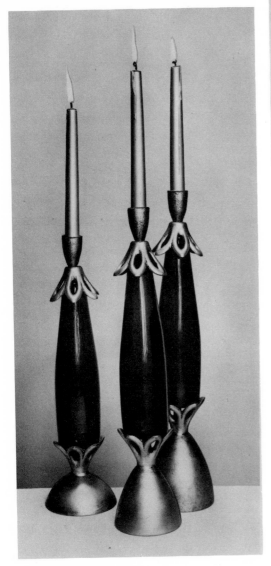

Fig. 285. Candle holders made of olive-green bottles, metal candle cups, and ceramic forms. The stands were cast in molds for matching sherbert dishes and tumblers. (A crown-shaped foot fits both pieces and was cast separately.) The bowls were poured to different levels to vary the heights of the stands, and the feet were attached while the clay was still damp. Three extra feet were cast for trimming the tops of the bottles. The greenware was cleaned, bisque-fired, and sprayed with flat black paint. High spots of stands, trim, and candle cups were rubbed with wax gilt, then the parts were assembled with epoxy, using strips of masking tape to hold them in place until the adhesive had set.

PLASTIC DISCARDS

As was observed earlier in the chapter, plastic containers are rapidly replacing glass in many areas of marketing. The shift derives from practical aspects of production, storage, and shipping, rather than aesthetic considerations, though a few manufacturers are beginning to recognize a need for designing forms which are less forthrightly utilitarian in appearance.

The glass enthusiast is inclined to regard plastic with a certain amount of scorn but in all fairness it must be admitted that plastic discards have a number of advantages over glass, particularly where budget limitations prohibit investing in special equipment. They are easily cut with shears or a sharp knife; parts can be joined with plastic adhesives and colored with plastic paints.[4] Since the hazard of sharp edges does not exist, plastic projects are safe for even the most inexperienced craftsman.

The most common plastic containers are made of *thermoplastic* compounds, which means that they can be repeatedly resoftened by heat. This has significance where the original form of the container does not figure in the new design. In other words, the container can be cut and reshaped over another form in the kitchen oven. It can also be sliced and flattened into sheets at low heat to make a raw material as basic as paper, cardboard, or tin.

[4] Labels on adhesives and paints should be checked to ascertain that they are recommended for plastic, since many products are unsuitable.

Figs. 287 and 288. Art Grant's provocative mobiles are evidence that with imagination, humble plastic discards can be vehicles for creative expression. Some memory of the original form is retained, though the relationship is elusive and often humorous. The slightest breeze sets "Fallen Angel" in motion, and new compositions are continuously created as the figures float around an invisible axis. It was cut in a single piece from a white plastic bowl as shown in Figure 288.

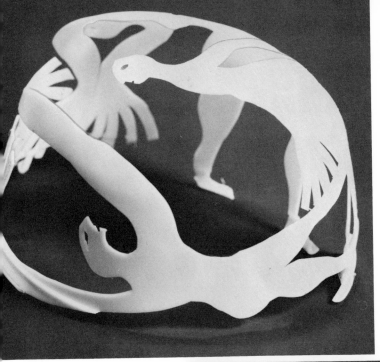

Fig. 289. "Blue Angel," by Art Grant, was cut from a plastic bottle.

Fig. 290. "Pink Ballerina" was originally the leg of a large plastic doll. Its derivation is apparent only upon close observation of the shape of her feet. By Art Grant.

Fig. 291. Christmas bells made from the upper portions of plastic containers for a laundry additive. The bottles were trimmed and sprayed with transparent paints. Bands of shaded yarn were glued on the tops and the decorations were finished with wooden beads and tassels.

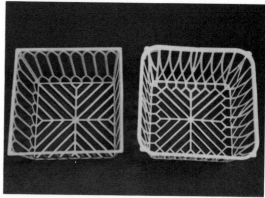

Fig. 292. Christmas ornaments can also be made from plastic baskets in which fruits and vegetables are packaged.

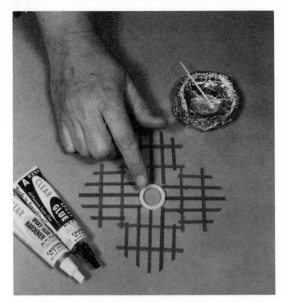

Fig. 293. The baskets are cut into interesting fragments and rejoined, using epoxy or a plastic adhesive. A curtain ring is glued in the center, partly as a design element and partly to strengthen the structure.

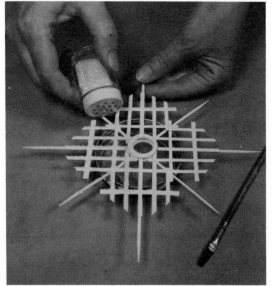

Fig. 294. Wooden hors d'oeuvre picks are added and the snowflake is sprayed white. It is then elevated on a jar lid and brushed with adhesive to secure an even sprinkling of white glitter.

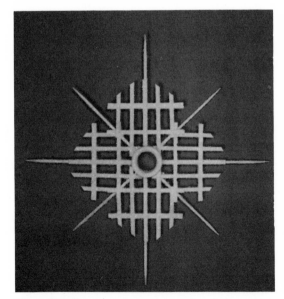

Fig. 295. This is but one example of the countless number of designs which can be made from baskets.

Fig. 296. Other possibilities are shown here. Children are inclined to make less symmetrical arrangements which are often even more interesting.

chapter 8

Bones, Stones, and Other Natural Materials

Man-made products are constantly changing as new needs arise from shifts in environmental patterns and as improved manufacturing processes are discovered. The products of nature are also constantly changing, though sometimes the alterations come about so slowly that it is hard to identify them as stages in a moving cycle.

The order of nature progresses inevitably from birth to maturity to death to birth again, each phase of growth and decay producing its marvels of textures and patinas.

Man's aesthetic response to these wonders is older than recorded history, as are his attempts to impose his own order on the designs of nature. His efforts have often been playful, motivated by impulses no more complex than a desire for self-adornment. Sometimes, however, they have grown from a deeper sensitivity: a search, perhaps, for the key to his own place in the scheme of things, or possibly from a determination to exercise some control over his own destiny.

We can imagine that the unknown craftsman who whittled the little fox in Figure 298 considered it to be a charm which would assure his prowess as a hunter, but it is also possible that he created it as a toy to amuse a child during the long, dark hours of an Arctic winter. Or maybe he simply found the material pleasant to work with and elected to carve a fox because its shape could be thriftily adapted to the shape of the walrus tusk.

Whatever stimulated his production, however, his action was preceded by his discovery of artistic value in the tusk itself. Ivory is so beautiful that such perception is not astonishing, but the capacity to appreciate the intrinsic beauty of ordinary animal bones, corn husks, and roadside stones is another matter.

It is, in fact, what this book is all about.

Fig. 297. Cornshuck doll by May Deschamp. (Photo by Edward DuPuy, courtesy of Southern Highland Handicraft Guild.)

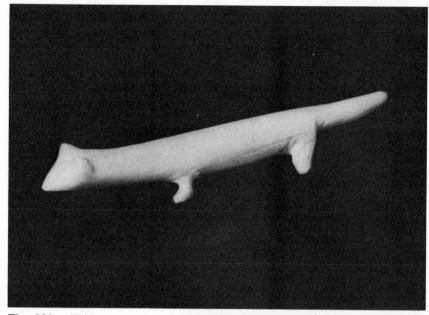

Fig. 298. Eskimo carving from walrus ivory. (Collection of the author.)

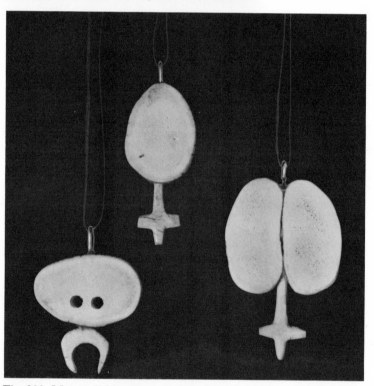

Fig. 299. Marcus White discovered the beautiful grain and colorations of sliced deer horn when he was teaching a group of children to make primitive ornaments. He works with very conventional equipment—a hacksaw, drill, and sander. The sections of his pendants are put together with tiny pegs and epoxy. He also assembles and carves small sculptures from table bones. (Photo by permission of Anima Mundi Gallery.)

Fig. 300. Alice Shannon is internationally famous for her jewelry made from gems and precious metals, but she is equally fascinated by the decorative qualities of bones and native stones. This exotic necklace combines seal's teeth, silver forms, silver beads, and Persian turquoise with the skull and jawbones of a wild goose. (Photo courtesy of the artist.)

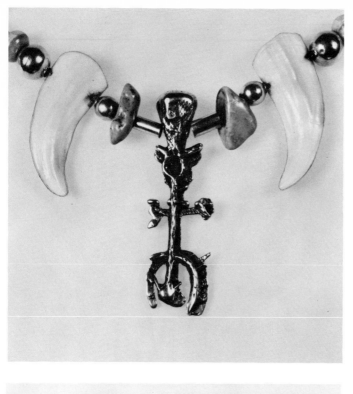

Fig. 301. The pendant in this example of her work (detail) was carved in cuttlebone and cast in silver. It is flanked by seal's teeth, chunks of turquoise, and silver beads.

Fig. 302. Turkey and chicken bones coated with satiny black acrylic paint are linked together with jet beads. By Alice Shannon.

Fig. 303. Sculpture by Alice Shannon. Carved cuttlebone cast in silver. (Photo courtesy of the artist.)

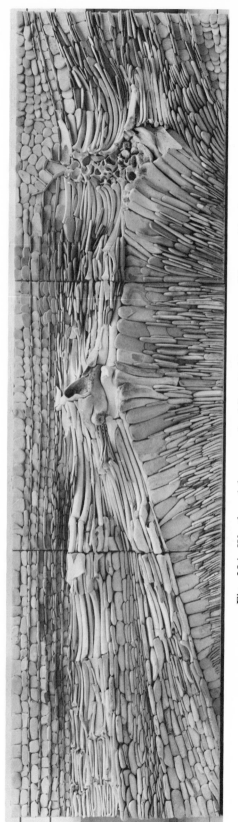

Fig. 304. Weathered bones and white stones are compatibly combined in "Triptych" by H. G. Pashigian. (Photo by Richard Gross, courtesy of California Design, Pasadena Art Museum.)

Fig. 305. "Bones #17." Robert McChesney was an established painter before his interest was diverted to three-dimensional compositions made of animal bones collected from the woods around his home. In his earlier pieces, the bones were left in their natural states or were painted flat black. Later he began to experiment with vibrant colors. His technique of assembly is meticulous and painstaking. The bones are first secured to a backing with adhesives, nails, or heavy staples. A shallow setting bed of polyester resin is then poured around the bones to lock them permanently in place. Sand, sisal, and a variety of discarded objects are sometimes included. (Photo by Marshall Douglas.)

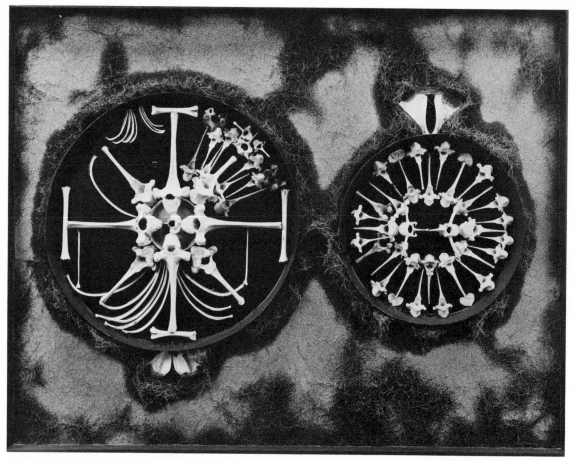

Fig. 306. "Estrellas de la Noche #1" by Robert McChesney. (Photo by Julian Williams.)

STONES

Stones have been carved, engraved, and painted from prehistoric times to the present. The early sculptures were largely dependent upon natural forms and craftsmen were content to suggest symbolic figures with a few sketchy alterations. Contemporary trends are also toward simple, uncluttered statements and their comparison with the crudely chiseled "Venuses" of the Old and New Stone Ages make it appear that we have made a full circle. We have moved from symbolism through naturalism and realism back to symbolism again.

Stone carving is certainly one technique for working with found materials, but it is less related to the general theme of this book than the processes used in the following examples. They illustrate several different approaches to creating designs from common boulders and beach pebbles without special equipment. Diversified though the goals and results might be, in all cases the basic shapes provided by nature are left unchanged.

Figs. 308, 309. Sally Wetherby adds nothing but paint to natural stones to create "minisculptures." The bottoms of the stones are slightly flattened with coarse sandpaper or an electric grinder, then the surface is sealed with varnish or polymer medium. Simple details that define subjects suggested by the basic shapes are delineated with washes of polymer paint and waterproof ink. The sculptures are finished with several coats of varnish.

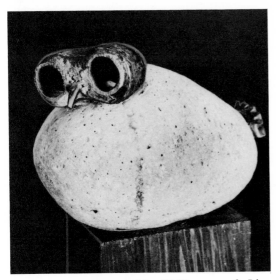

Fig. 307. The remarkable lifelikeness of Lino Pera's "Thrush" was achieved with only a pitted boulder, a double pipe joint, a pointed bit of metal, and a segment of a brass gear.

Fig. 310. "Reunion." Maggie Jagla's pebble pictures are humorous illustrations of familiar scenes. They are composed of natural stones and bits of shells that are secured with white glue to fabric-covered backings. Her ideas start with a pebble that reminds her of something. She builds the story from there, often sifting through thousands of stones to find a shape which is exactly right.

Fig. 311. "Waiting Room" by Maggie Jagla. This concept of illustration could readily be adapted for use in classrooms and childrens' summer recreational programs. Aside from its economical aspect, it combines the fun of storytelling with that of putting things together to make a picture. Seeds, cone petals, and chips of driftwood could also be added to the stones.

SAND PAINTINGS

Indian sand paintings were originally made by medicine men as part of their religious ceremonies. By skillfully controlling the flow of varicolored sands from their cupped hands, they drew elaborate symbols on the ground through which they summoned the spirits of the gods.

For many years, duplication of the traditional designs was not permitted. Recently, however, to preserve these important elements of their ancient culture, contemporary Indian artists have begun to recreate them in permanent form by setting the sands in adhesives. Fine examples of this work are shown in Figures 312, 313, and 314. Natural colors usually include ochre, browns, white, and metallic black, though sometimes touches of finely ground turquoise of grades too poor for jewelry are added.

Designs for sand paintings should be kept fairly simple, and it is practical to work on a backing of colored matboard or sandpaper glued to heavy cardboard, pressed hardboard, or plywood. This not only eliminates the tedium of filling in the background, but makes it possible to obtain dimensional contrast with elevated sandy trails and solid areas.

The sand is prepared by sifting it through a very fine strainer or one thickness of nylon stocking material. Soft rocks can be pulverized into sand by pounding them with a hammer on a concrete surface. For variety, small quantities of dry mortar pigments can be added to basic sand colors. Colored batches should be tested on a scrap of backing material, for some of the dark pigments (such as black and cobalt blue) will stain matboard and become so firmly lodged in the crevices of coarse sandpaper that they cannot be brushed out.

For classroom purposes, a single light color of sand and a choice of several dark backings can be provided.

A design is sketched lightly on the sandpaper and small areas of one color at a time are coated with white glue, using a toothpick to spread it smoothly right up to the outlines. The sand is sifted into the wet adhesive and after the glue is dry, the board is turned over and tapped to dislodge unattached particles.

Several coats of matte-finish varnish sprayed on the finished painting will contribute to its permanence.

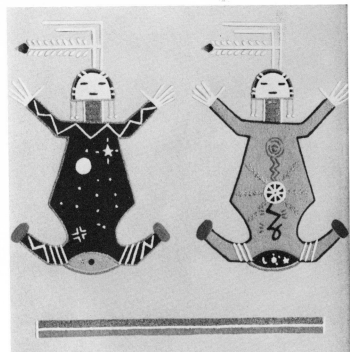

Fig. 312. "Mother Earth and Father Sky." Traditional symbols that were used in ancient rituals are being preserved in sand paintings by contemporary Indian artists. The three examples here are by Wilson Price of New Mexico. The dark figure in this design is Mother Earth; the lighter figure is Father Sky.

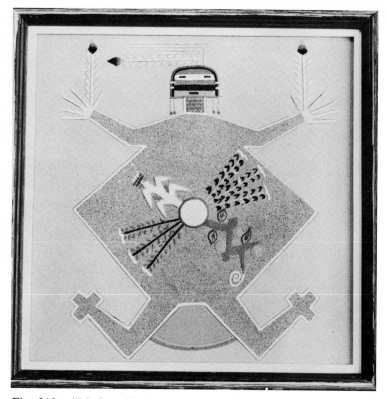

Fig. 313. "Mother Earth."
Mother Earth is personified
as the source of the seeds of
all living things, and this ver-
sion shows life-giving energy
of the sun radiating from her
bosom.

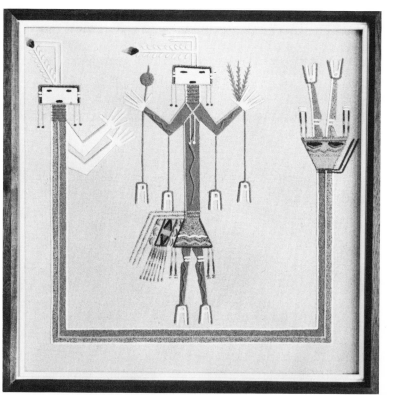

Fig. 314. "Yei and Rain-
bow." Yei were considered
intermediaries between man
and God, and supplications
for their aid often accompanied special rituals for
treating an ailing member of
the tribe. The central figure
of the yei here is female.
(Male yei are represented
with round heads.) She is
surrounded by a rainbow
guardian. (Sand paintings
photographed by permission
of YAH-A-TEH.)

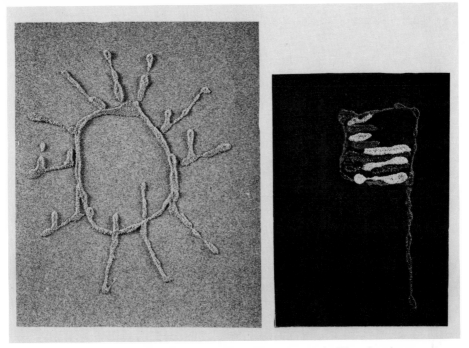

Fig. 315. "Sun" and "Flag" by Wendy Sestak, age 6. Glue drawings on sandpaper, sifted with colored sand.

EARTH PAINTINGS

The Cro-Magnon earth paintings show such a high level of accomplishment that for many years after they were discovered critics believed them to be fradulent. It was only after similar examples were found in widely scattered regions that skeptics were forced to give due credit to men who lived thirty thousand or more years ago.

The survival of these cave paintings say all that is necessary about the permanence of earth pigments and the simplicity of equipment needed to work with them. In addition, the texture and limited palette of low-key colors have a character that is entirely different from other painting media.

Earth with a high clay content makes the best paint. Sand and plant matter should be sieved out. Dry mortar pigments can be added for color variety but they should be used with discretion. They are highly concentrated and can become so dominant that the earthy quality is lost. The old cave paintings prove the effectiveness of using varying intensities of only one or two colors.

Polymer (acrylic) mediums or varnishes are excellent vehicles for making earth into paint. The mix can be thin for detailed brushwork, or thick for freer application with a pallette knife. Since the mediums are milky, the colors appear to be somewhat bland when they are first mixed, but the cloudiness disappears as they dry.

Fig. 316. Pablita Velarde is one of the best-known contemporary Indian artists, and her fine craftsmanship is evident in these two versions of "Hump-Backed Flute Player and Bear Tracks." The designs are painted with colored clays mixed with oils and other binding agents. The velvety "tooth" of earth paintings is quite unlike the granular texture of sand painting. (Photos by permission of YAH-A-TEH.)

GRAVEL PICTURES

Gravel pictures are made by essentially the same process as sand paintings, but the larger size of the granules dictates the need for designs of a proportionately larger scale. It is a good idea to establish outlines first and fill in between them after the glue is dry. Ribbons of gravel can be glued down for this purpose, as can other fragmented materials which are compatible. Beach pebbles were used for outlines in "Summer Flowers," shown in the color section. For designs of a more formalized nature such as Figure 317, heavy string, cording, or yarn makes crisper borders. To avoid monotony in the linear pattern, the separate segments of "Flower Wheel" were delineated by one to four rows of cotton rug yarn.

Once the outlines were established and dry, a bed of white glue about $\frac{1}{16}$-inch thick was spread inside one section of the design. A layer of gravel was sprinkled into the glue and tamped down firmly with the back of a spoon. The color areas in Figure 317 are flat. For the shaded effects in "Summer Flowers," harmonious colors of gravel were sprinkled on top of the base layer.

As each section was completed, a solution of one part glue and two parts water was trickled over the gravel until it was completely saturated. The liquid was distributed with a soft brush and extra granules were added where necessary. After the completed design had cured about a week, it was sprayed with several thin coats of satin-finish varnish.

Fig. 317. "Flower Wheel" by Mary Lou Stribling. From a short distance away the texture of gravel resembles petit point. In geometric designs, color areas can be crisply separated by outlines of cording, rope, or yarn. Natural colors can be varied to some extent by flooding glued-down sections with polymer paints diluted with polymer medium. Dyed gravels are also produced commercially for use in aquariums as well as crafts. (See Index of Supplies.)

Fig. 318. The design for this gravel mural for a child's room was developed from an adaptation of a child's drawing of a zebra. The outlines of black gravel were attached first with white glue, then other areas were filled in one section at a time. By Joan Goldstein.

SEEDS

Seeds for decorative projects should be heated in the oven to prevent germination and to kill any insect eggs or larvae. Most hard seeds can be colored with hot concentrated solutions of fabric dyes if they are handled quickly. If they are left submerged too long, they may swell or partially disintegrate.

Only hard, clean, dry seeds should be used since roasted seeds may have glazes of salt or other preservatives which will resist absorption of the color. To dye seeds, 1 teaspoon powdered dye is dissolved in ½ cup of hot water. The solution is brought to a boil and removed from heat. A small amount of seeds is immediately dropped in and stirred for 30 to 60 seconds, or until color develops to the desired intensity. Seeds are poured into a strainer over a container so that the dye can be reserved, then scattered on several layers of paper towels. Puddles of color are absorbed when they are rolled around a few times.

MAKING A SEED MOSAIC

Fig. 319. A framed pressed hardboard backing is painted dark brown, and the top edge of the frame is covered with masking tape to protect it from glue splashes. The basic lines of the design are drawn on the backing with chalk or white pencil.

Fig. 320. Starting with the center of one of the flowers, whole cloves are arranged in a band of white glue, using a toothpick to push them closely together.

Fig. 321. The clove circlet is filled with dyed popcorn set in one grain at a time with sharp tips slanted downward the way they grow on the cob. Dyed sunflower seeds around the border of the flower are arranged slightly overlapping, like shingles.

Fig. 322. Working from the outer border to the center, two rows of dyed popcorn are attached, then the remaining spaces are coated with glue and packed with natural mustard seeds. The finished flower head is saturated with diluted glue.

Fig. 323. Edges of the large flowers are trimmed with popcorn, then small flowers are formed from sunflower seeds and popcorn. After the popcorn stems are secured, whole allspice is glued on the vertical lines of the background. Strips are filled alternately with brown coriander seeds and whole black peppercorns. Diluted white glue is brushed over the finished panel. (See "Garden Fence" in the color section.)

MISCELLANEOUS NATURAL MATERIALS

Fig. 324. Peruvian craftsmen make many things from gourds, including covered boxes, bowls, and figures of fish, animals, birds, and people. Subjects are often suggested by the natural shapes of the gourds, though sometimes scenes from everyday life are incised or burned on the surface.

Fig. 325. Household gods of the Marshall Islands carved from the smoky pearl lining of a shell.

HILLS OF MARIN. By Mary Lou Stribling. Lava rock, marble cubes, pebbles, Byzantine smalti, and scraps of frame molding set in colored magnesite. (*Collection of Mr. and Mrs. Kendall Curry.*)

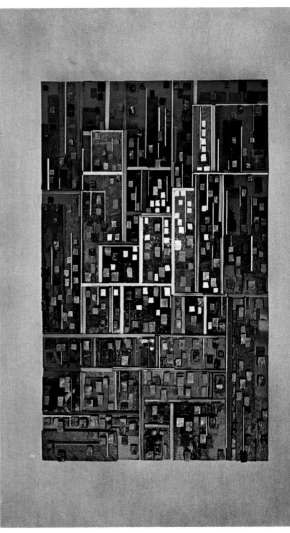

THE LATE CITY. By Mary Lou Stribling. Layered scraps of salvaged glass and Byzantine smalti.

THE SUN. By Charlotte Patera. Appliquéd cotton remnants.

SOPHISTICATED PRIMITIVE. By Charlotte Patera. Reverse appliqué hanging of assorted cotton scraps.

CRYING CHIMES. By Mary Lou Stribling. Clock parts and salvaged brass rods.

TREE BONES. By Mary Lou Stribling. Driftwood, pebbles, and water-worn brick nuggets.

FIVE FLOWERS. By Ann Hunt. Salvaged glass colored on the subsurface with opaque copper enamels. (*Photograph courtesy of the artist.*)

Fig. 326. PRESSED FLOWER MINIATURES FROM KOREA

Many leaves and flowers will retain their natural colors to some degree if they are picked at their prime and dried between sheets of absorbent papers under a weight. For best results, plants should not be stacked or overlapped, and the papers should be changed every few days to prevent mildew. When they are thoroughly dry, they can be attached to white or tinted matboard with tiny dots of paste or white glue. Fragile materials of this kind should be protected by covers of glass or plastic.

Fig. 327. For designs more contemporary in style, heavier leaves and flowers can be handled in an entirely different way. These are glued to individual rectangles of stained balsa wood, then sealed with five or six coats of matte polymer medium for permanent protection. They are attached to a plywood backing using ⅛-inch strips of balsa to visually frame each motif. Chapter 10 includes techniques for making impressions from similar materials.

chapter 9

Mixed Media and Miscellany

Design is an important element in all art activities, but we have now come to an area of found art where restraint, selectivity, and organization have special significance.[1]

No unusual problems are involved in uniting the elements of compositions made from one kind of material or from objects which are similar in nature, since a certain relatedness automatically exists. However, there is often no natural harmony among the ingredients of mixed-media designs and order must be achieved by judicious planning.

One technique for unifying an assemblage of assorted objects is to obscure distracting colors and textures with paint, gesso, plaster, or siftings of sand or sawdust, so that interest will be focused on patterns created by elevations and shadows. Many artists have used this device with great success as evidenced by Picasso's sculpture, "Construction with Glove (By the Sea)," Figure 6; Mary Case Dekker's

[1] The word "design" is used here in its meaning of "plan," and does not refer to the process of drawing a motif or pattern.

reliefs in Figures 328, 337, and 344; and the relief paintings by Richard Sorby in Figures 338 and 339.

An alternate approach might be compared to deliberately mixing a formula for a potion which will produce a certain effect. But before the artist can work out the proper proportions of the various ingredients in his mixture, he must decide which materials are strong and which are weak.

The judgment starts with evaluation of their visual characteristics to establish what might be called their *attention quotients*. This is not necessarily related to native beauty, which may be apparent only when materials are studied separately or at close range. But their position on the attention scale will be determined by their eye appeal in relation to the other objects around them. In other words, we are not concerned with deciding that one substance is aesthetically superior to another, but rather with which will attract the greatest interest. This will provide a guideline for plotting the focus of the design.

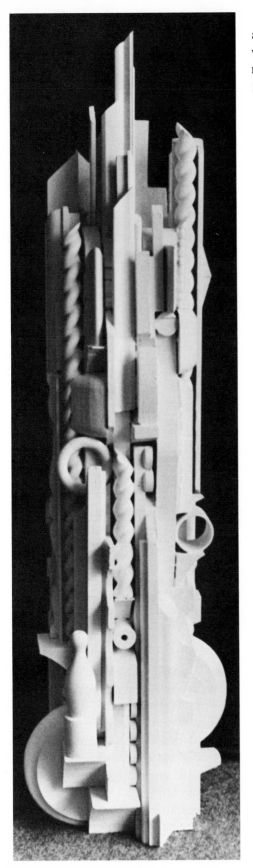

The focus of a composition could be defined as its center of activity. The eye will follow what it finds exciting, even to the point of ignoring more intellectually worthwhile visions in its immediate vicinity. Sights which are ugly, shocking, startling, infuriating, or revolting are as eye-catching as those which are pleasing. Perhaps even more so. That leaves us with but one reaction which will not be tolerated: *boredom.*

Different things are boring to different people, but monotony is boring to nearly everyone. Monotony in an art work can result from triteness or inept craftsmanship, but it can also be caused by a lack of contrast. To put it another way, a design is monotonous when the attention quotients of all elements are equal.

Being aware of this pitfall is half the battle. The other half consists of supplementing instinct with analytical know-how so that when a design suddenly "goes limp," its ailment can be diagnosed and a cure prescribed to set it in motion again.

Every artist eventually works out his own diagnostic techniques, but both problems and solutions can be found in the following elements of basic design.[2]

LINE

Let us imagine now that we are looking from a window at a distant landscape of rolling hills. If there is a road winding up one hill, our eyes will immediately follow it, and we may feel vaguely disturbed if it continues to lead us away from the view. *Line,* then, is one element of design which can be utilized to contain attention within a given area. Linear movement

[2] Comments on design theory are of necessity brief, and are not intended to replace more detailed study.

Fig. 328. "White City" by Mary Case Dekker. Wood turnings, scraps of molding, spools, wooden curtain rings, toys, and segments of fiberboard tubing are attached with white glue to a 4-by-4-inch wooden post and sprayed flat white. (Photo courtesy of the artist.)

can also set the pace of a composition, which has a direct bearing on its impact. Straight lines move fast, and speed is exciting. Curved lines are more leisurely and restful. Meandering lines move slowest of all and contribute to an atmosphere of tranquility.

In "Low Tide," Figure 330, the essential mass is a large circular form which represents a crusty shell on a beach. The radiating lines around the center of the mass move quickly outward, but before we are carried beyond the boundaries of the frame, we are caught by the inward sweep of water at the lower right. The trailing edge of a wave leads us upward and back down again to the center.

Fig. 329. Cement setting beds for exterior mosaics should be from 1 to 1½ inches thick. Slow-setting compounds are best, and they can be lightened by additions of vermiculite, perlite, or powdered asbestos. Tacks hammered partly into the backing will lock the cement to the foundation. Large panels require the additional reinforcement of a layer of coarse screening.

Fig. 330. "Low Tide" was built up one section at a time as described for "Hills of Marin" in Chapter 5. Materials include wooden rods, chunks of driftwood bark, beach pebbles, broken shells, smalti, and scraps of gold-backed cathedral glass. By Mary Lou Stribling.

TEXTURE

A comprehensive arrangement of *textures* can be tricky, especially where a number of distinctly textured materials are involved. The materials in "Tree Bones," Figure 198, are not really alike, but their natural harmonious colors and worn, rounded contours give them a certain kinship. Textural variety was obtained by arranging the fragments in graduated sizes.

The same basic composition would be drastically changed by the inclusion of glittering chunks of glass, and the placement of the particles would have to be skillfully plotted to avoid "busyness." Shiny or faceted surfaces are more eye-catching than mat or smooth surfaces, so if the glass were scattered at random in the background, our eyes would simply jump from bright spot to bright spot until they were bored by the monotony of the motion.

Linear rhythms and textures in the bas-re-

Fig. 331. Helen Steinau Rich does not draw a detailed cartoon for her mosaics, but works instead from simple sketches that indicate light and dark values and essential lines in the composition. Three-dimensional planes are modeled in magnesite, and decorative materials are pressed into it while the cement is still plastic.

lief mosaics by Helen Rich, Figures 331, 332, 333, 334, are complex but they have been so admirably organized that they are exciting, rather than exhausting.

The rugged texture of the bird in "Golden Crown Crane" results from overlapping the tesserae, like shingles, so that the figure stands out sharply against the flatter planes of the background. The glint of pebbled gold glass catches the eye here and there among the feathers, becoming bolder near the crown. The glass is streaked narrowly in the vertical lines behind the bird, then thickly encrusted in the tail feathers. The smooth flow of background tiles and a few crisp lines of hammered copper serve to stabilize the vibrating patterns.

Fig. 332. Thick copper wire pounded into irregular ribbons provides a crisp contrast to the rugged textures of "Golden Crown Crane." Other materials are beach glass, pebbles, abalone shells, smalti, and Venetian tiles. (Collection of Mr. and Mrs. Harold Freemon. Photos by Neville Rich.)

Fig. 333. "Molecular Fantasy," by Helen Rich, is an exotic combination of azurite, Brazilian garnet, obsidian, copper ore, hammered copper strips, pebbles, mirror glass from Thailand, bottle glass, smalti, and assorted pieces of hardware, some of which are deeply recessed. The theme was inspired by drawings of molecules of tungsten and other physics symbols. (Collection of Dr. and Mrs. Theodore Geballe.)

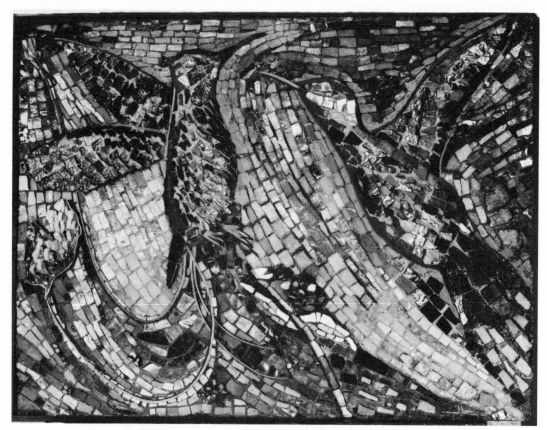

Fig. 334. "Hummingbirds." Mixed-media mosaic by Helen Rich. (Collection of Dr. and Mrs. Frederick Wolff.)

VOLUME

Volume, or the amount of space allotted to different materials in the composition, can also be used as a focalizing device. The scale and placement of the assorted components of "Psychedelic Dream," Figure 335, are interesting from a design standpoint, but beyond that, the work casts a tantalizing spell which provokes almost endless interpretations.

We are drawn first to the large head near the center, then we are compelled to examine the fascinating collection of objects in the separate "rooms" around it. Inexorably and repeatedly our eyes go back to the head. Size alone does not entirely account for this. The forms are subtly positioned to direct attention inward, rather than outward.

The dismembered torso at the upper left places the weight of interest in the lower part of the frame. Moving farther downward, we follow the serpentine half-frame to the projecting arm which curves toward the head. The undulating shapes in the box below the head might lead us out of the picture, but we are stopped by a leg which points inward, and curving lines which move upward. The disk in the next box is tilted slightly on its stem away from the edge of the frame. At the upper right, the hand reaches toward a mysterious lock and we are forced back to the focal point of the composition again.

Fig. 335. "Psychedelic Dream" by Harry Dix. (Photo by Nathan Rabin, courtesy of Bertha Schaefer Gallery.)

COLOR

Color can not only contain our interest within the framework of a composition, but it can vitally influence its *mood,* for we respond emotionally as well as intellectually to color, and our responses are extremely individualistic.

The most important quality of a color in its relation to other colors around it is its *value.* That is, its position on the scale from white to black. It is sometimes difficult to determine why a color pattern lacks sparkle without making a value analysis. A black-and-white photograph of the piece will often suggest where the weakness lies.

There is a classic assumption that hot colors come forward and cold colors recede, but like most classic assumptions, it should be preceded by the word *"usually."* An exception can be observed in the bone construction by Robert McChesney in the color section.

The size and elevation of the light yellow form contributes to its importance, but the fact that it is lighter in value than the surrounding masses is more significant. Had the values been reversed, the form would have been greatly diminished and its lines partially absorbed by the light behind them.

Value contrasts are as important in purely decorative designs as they are in works of more serious intention. "Summer Flowers" and "Garden Fence" in the color section are examples of how they can add dimension and luminosity to simple, stylized compositions.

SPECIAL TECHNIQUES FOR MIXED MEDIA COMPOSITIONS

The vivid assemblages of Alfonso Ossorio include such wildly unrelated objects as shells, antlers, artificial eyes, and junk jewelry. From a distance, one is caught by the shift of textures and colors, and the disturbing restlessness of contrasting rhythms. A closer view allows intimate recognition of the separate materials and the experience is delightful and unexpected.

He builds upon shapes of plywood, pressed hardboard, wood, or plastic, sometimes layering them to create caves and mazes. Brilliant colors or sandy aggregates are incorporated into his setting beds and adhesives, unifying the elements into solid glistening masses.

Ossorio's works are highly sophisticated, yet like the primitive craftsman who creates awesome fetishes from a ragtag collection of feathers, bones, and hides, he has an indescribable gift for breathing life into inanimate objects. The spirits which peer out from their secret places in his assemblages are no doubt benevolent, but their magic is potent, nevertheless.

The ethereal translucence of Bob Graham's "Cathedral" is unfortunately lost in a photograph. The basic material is scrap sheet acetate cut into elongated triangles, trapezoids, and arches, perforated at random with paper punches, and streaked lightly with dull gold ink. Multiple layers of the prepared strips are impaled on a soft pressed-board backing with red, yellow, blue, black, and white map pins in two sizes. Many of the "eyes" cut out by the punches are threaded on the pins, along with small squares and rectangles of red, yellow, and blue acetate. The shadow patterns and overlapping images create an illusion of remarkable depth.

The assorted elements of Wilma Harris's mixed media compositions are secured by an unusual technique of sand casting.[3] A deep box is filled with damp sand up to about two inches from the top and the decorative materials are pressed deeply into it. A quantity of cement sufficient to make a layer about an inch thick is mixed to a fairly fluid consistency and poured over the sand and protruding tips of the objects. When it has set, it is covered with a

---

[3] Detailed instructions for sand-casting are outlined in *Mosaic Techniques* by Mary Lou Stribling (New York: Crown Publishers, Inc., 1966).

Fig. 336. Alfonso Ossorio's "Halcyon" (shown here before it was framed) is a part of the permanent art collection of the New York Hilton Hotel. The assemblage is 4 feet in diameter and is composed of assorted bones, shells, mirrors, glass eyes, junk jewelry, chains, and other discards. (Photo by John Reed, courtesy of the New York Hilton Hotel.)

Fig. 337. "Composition in Silver and Black" by Mary Case Dekker. Wood blocks, old wood type, molding scraps, rubber stamps, and plastic and cardboard letters were attached to a wood backing with white glue then sprayed silver. Black acrylic paint was applied over the silver and rubbed from the high spots. Numbers and letters were printed on some of the blocks with toy rubber stamps. (Photo courtesy of the artist.)

Fig. 338. "Utah Forms" by J. Richard Sorby. A relief painting built up with water putty, broken strips of plywood, and pottery shards gathered along the Pacific Coast. The pink-orange sand from Utah that inspired the title was sifted onto glue in all the lower levels, predominating over the earth colors and providing textural interest.

Fig. 339. "Mesa," by J. Richard Sorby, was inspired by the form relationships of two broken automobile pistons. The pistons were fastened rigidly to a pressed-board backing with wire and invisible screws before the addition of found packing materials, old washers, and punched out metal pieces. Water putty, sand, vinyl glue, and matte acrylic medium were used with acrylic colors to complete the construction. The painting was basically abstract in concept until a title was decided upon, but the holes in the pistons suggested cliff dwellings even when the artist first found them in a junk yard.

Fig. 340. "Cathedral," by Bob Graham, is made of layered scraps of sheet acetate and assorted map pins. (Collection of Mr. and Mrs. C. K. Patera.)

Fig. 341. A closer view of the composition reveals the intricacy of the translucent patterns and the jewellike texture created by the tiny dots and squares of color.

reinforcing sheet of coarse screening and a second, denser layer of cement. Perlite, powdered asbestos, vermiculite, and other similar aggregates are often added to the basic cement mixture to reduce the weight of the panel.

The slab is covered with damp newspapers and placed in a cool area to dry slowly. It is then lifted from the box and loose sand is brushed away from the surface.

For small indoor panels, she sometimes follows the same procedure, using plaster of Paris instead of cement. Where delicate impressions are combined with found objects, she substitues light cooking oil for water as a moistening agent for the sand. This not only enables her to make sharper imprints, but also allows her to work on the piece as long as she likes without the bother of keeping the sand damp. The oiled sand can be reused indefinitely.

Fig. 342. "Constellation." Mixed-media sand casting by Wilma Harris. A black cork float, blue bottle bottom, green reflector light, broken tiles, pebbles, and other found materials were arranged upside down with design reversed, on a bed of damp sand. They were pressed in deeply, leaving enough surface extending to lock into the layer of mortar. A creamy mixture of cement, sand, lightweight aggregate, and water, reinforced with hardware cloth, formed the permanent slab.

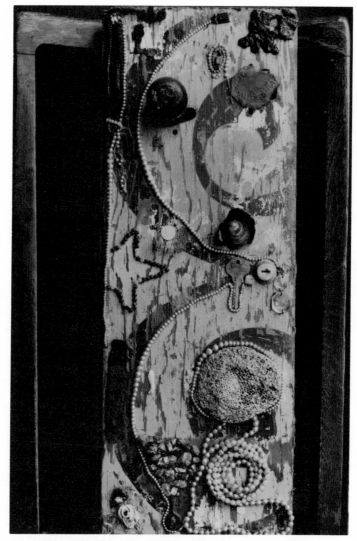

Fig. 343. "My Beach" by Maude Lynne. Old
beads, shells, rocks, and assorted beach treasures
attached to a weathered, discarded wardrobe door.
(Photo by permission of Sankey Gallery.)

MISCELLANEOUS MATERIALS

Vicious and macabre figures appear to be bursting from the orderly compartments of "Children's Games" by Mary Case Dekker. The figures in the foreground are obviously engaged in combat. Some are watchfully alert; others stalk, jab, or aim at an unseen enemy. Skeletons and grinning skulls peer over their shoulders.

Near the center of the composition, a symbol of death occupies his own private cell. Below it is a crucifix.

The depth of this protest against war and violence is not fully realized until the identity of the materials becomes evident. They are all toys manufactured for the purpose of providing children with things to play with in their spare time. Some of the figures, including the "Grim Reaper," are bonuses tucked into boxes of cereal, confections, and snacks. Others were created from a kit which is designed to enable children to cast and heat-cure plastic forms in prepared molds.

The assemblage is dedicated to the artist's young nephew who was killed in Vietnam.

Fig. 344. "Children's Games (For Billy)" (detail) by Mary Case Dekker. Toy soldiers, plastic forms created from a kit for children, and prizes from boxes of cereal and candy, set in an old type tray. The assemblage is finished with flat black paint.

Fig. 345. This intriguingly tortuous sculpture appears to be welded metal, but it is actually made of plastic margins and rods left over from airplane and boat model kits. David Eckels, who made the sculpture when he was fourteen, fused the pieces together by melting the joints slightly with a wood-burning tool, then painted the construction flat black. From this angle, the subject could be an exuberant musician plucking an equally exuberant stringed instrument.

Fig. 346. "Melody" by Ann Griffith. Wire and salvaged parts of an old piano.

Fig. 347. Florence Packard salvages interesting forms for earrings, pendants, and cuff links from unfired pottery which is accidentally chipped or cracked. Using the curvature of the greenware as part of her design, she cuts out irregular shapes, smooths the edges, and pierces any necessary holes.

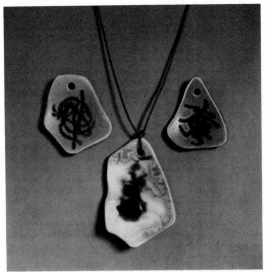

Fig. 348. The pieces are then decorated and completed in a single firing. The two upper pendants were finished with muted, semi-matte glazes on which glass threads (used for copper enameling) were scattered at random. The large central pendant has a chunk of broken glass melted into a frosty-green art glaze.

Fig. 349. "The Glad Eye," a centrifugal casting by Alice Shannon. The sterling silver hair ornament is set with a glass eye. A hand-carved ebony stick holds the ornament in place.

Fig. 350. "Eyelashes" by Alice Shannon. Yellow gold ring set with a glass eye.

chapter 10

Prints, Patterns, and Impressions

Up to this point, our attention has been directed toward the positive face of found art. That is, we have examined techniques for incorporating the actual substance of objects and materials into works which may or may not be related to the original substance as far as subject matter is concerned. The negative face, or the *image* of found materials is fully as interesting and deserves a great deal more exploration than remaining space permits.

STAMPED DESIGNS

Bark cloth has been made in many tropical countries from a number of different kinds of plants, but it is generally agreed that the Polynesian tapa [1] is superior to that produced anywhere else. The Hawaiians in particular excelled in the manufacture of tapa (or kapa)

and developed a variety of unique processes, patterns, and dyes.

Bark from the paper mulberry shrub was a favorite raw material, and the basic technique of cleaning, softening, and pounding the fibers into pliable sheets appears to be the same throughout Polynesia. The Hawaiians, however, added a distinctive element to their kapa by using patterned beaters during the final stages of refining the cloth, thereby texturing it with decorative watermarks.

Older methods of decorating finished sheets of bark cloth included dyeing by immersion, by freehand painting, or by making multiple rubbings of some textured surface. Tahitian and Fijian tapa makers dipped leaves, bamboo tubes, and other found objects in dye and used them as stamps to create designs, but only the

---

[1] Tapa is the Polynesian word for non-woven cloth made from the pulp or bark of various shrubs and plants, but it may be pronounced and spelled differently in different dialects. Bark cloth made by the Hawaiians is called "kapa." The Samoan word is "siapo," and the Fijian word is "masi." Other syllables may be added to the base words to describe special kinds of tapa which are dark, thin, waterproof, and so on.

Hawaiians developed a true process of block printing. The technique is remarkably sophisticated, even by today's standards of hand craftsmanship, but the accomplishment is even more remarkable when it is evaluated against the Stone Age culture from which it evolved.

Tapa making completely disappeared in Hawaii when machine-made fabrics became available, but the craft is still alive in some of the other Polynesian islands. Unfortunately, except for an occasional rare find, most examples of contemporary bark cloth lack the quality of design and workmanship of the earlier products.

The deterioration should not be attributed to a decrease of talent among the islanders, but rather to an increase of commerce. The tourist's dollars have elevated living conditions in many parts of the world, but sadly enough, his enthusiasm for souvenirs has also contributed to an increasing disregard for fine craftsmanship.

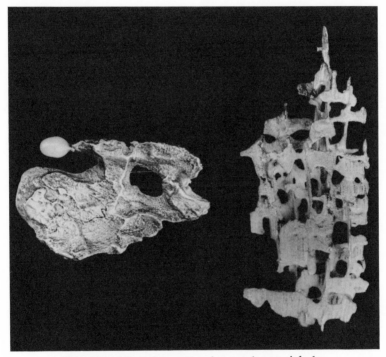

Fig. 351. Silver burnouts of natural materials by Alice Shannon. The brooch on the left has a white Biwa pearl and was made from a fragment of unrefined cork. The brooch on the right is a burnout of a piece of decayed wood.

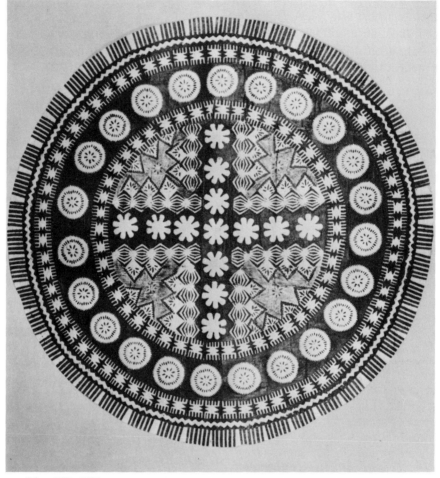

Fig. 352. Fijian tapa. Bark cloth was originally produced for utilitarian purposes in cultures which had not developed the art of woven fabrics. The cloth was decorated with dyes, rubbings, painted designs, and printed patterns from natural materials. (Collection of the author.)

Fig. 353. Tapa from New Hebrides, Melanesia. Crude brushes were used to distribute paint over large areas. Delineating accents were sometimes made with sticks, edges of shells, bones, and the circular ends of cut bamboo. (Photo courtesy of the M. H. De Young Memorial Museum.)

Fig. 354. Hawaiian tapa was of superior quality, and had many refinements which distinguished it from the bark cloth made in other Polynesian islands. Textured beaters impressed a watermark on the fabric before it was colored. (Photo courtesy of the Bernice P. Bishop Museum.)

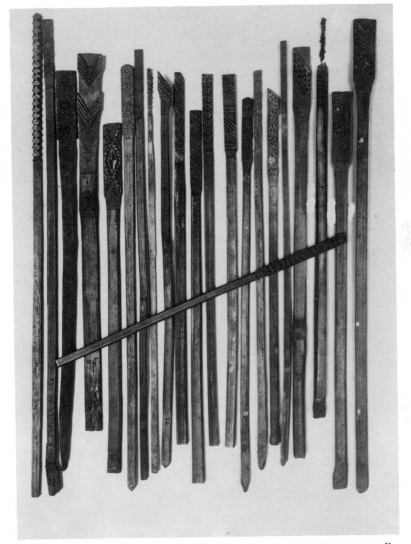

Fig. 355. Found objects were used to stamp early tapa, but eventually, Hawaiians discovered how to carve printing stamps on the flat sides of lengths of sliced bamboo. The markers were dipped into dye and pressed on the cloth in the same way that we use rubber stamps today. (Photo courtesy of the Bernice P. Bishop Museum.)

Fig. 356. More than one motif was often used in the all-over repeat patterns of Hawaiian tapa, but as demonstrated here, several different designs could be obtained from a single marker. Other variations resulted from alternating or superimposing colors. Keys, spools, washers, and other found objects may similarly be arranged in many different ways. (Photo courtesy of the Bernice P. Bishop Museum.)

Figs. 357, 358. The highly decorative quality of early tapa patterns has inspired many designers of contemporary fabrics and wrapping papers. For the most part, colors are brown, black, and creamy white, though artists often depart from tradition by using other combinations.

Fig. 359. Stamps as simple as three strips of balsa glued to a spool will make a number of different printed patterns. Water-soluble printing inks eliminate the chore of cleaning brushes and tools with special solvents. An ink pad for rubber stamps is handy for testing resilient materials, such as potatoes, corks, sink stoppers, and flexible washers.

Fig. 360. Clearest prints from rigid objects are obtained by applying oil paints or printing inks to the stamp with a brush, particularly where the objects are not perfectly level. The application will be smoother on metals and other hard materials if a bit of soap is added to water-soluble colors. Graduations in intensity of the colors result when several printings are made without recoating the stamp.

Fig. 361. Spools and corks can be used both as stamps and as handles for flat objects. A large spool, corks, a staple glued to a cork, and a metal gear are shown in the top row, with their stamped patterns beneath them. In the bottom row are stampings from nail heads and a sink stopper.

Fig. 362. These motifs illustrate a few of the possible combinations of prints from the objects in Figure 361, in one- and two-color stampings.

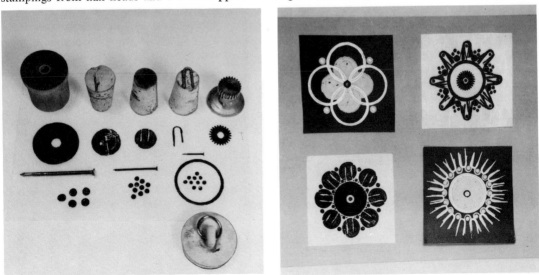

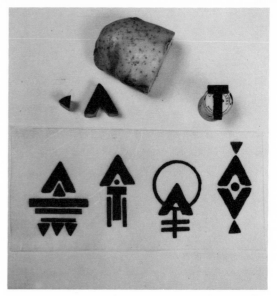

Fig. 363. Potato prints have been classic school art projects for many years. In addition to the usual technique of incising designs on the potato, it can be cut into shaped blocks, either by hand or with cutters for cookies and canapés.

Fig. 364. A triangular block was cut from a slice of potato, then notched to make the two stamps at the upper left. The stamp at the upper right is two strips of balsa glued to a spool. The motifs at the bottom are combinations of these elements, along with some of the stamps in Figure 361.

Fig. 365. The pattern on the left was made from a gear, nail heads, and the rim of a canapé cutter. On the right, the scalloped potato stamp in Figure 363, corks, and nail heads were used to print the flower. Circles and half circles were printed with a sink stopper.

Fig. 366. The design potential in stamps made from potatoes, keys, sliced shells, and other found objects is almost inexhaustible. They provide a rich source of inspiration for creating motifs for ceramics, embroidery, and appliqué.

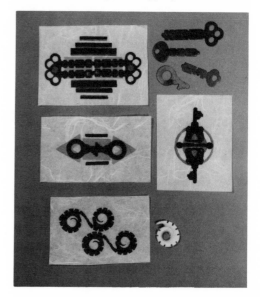

INDIRECT PAINTINGS

Monopainting is a combination of techniques for printmaking and those of traditional painting. Paint is not applied directly onto the final ground, but is spread first on other surfaces and transferred by pressure to the permanent base. Several separate prints are often overlaid to build up the composition, producing textures and images which could not be obtained by other methods.

As a start, crumpled cellophane, crepe paper, string, raveled jute, and the like can be glued to cardboard to make printing blocks. The blocks are rolled with oil paints or block printing inks and pressed against sheets of paper to study the characteristic textures and veining produced by each material.

Paints can also be applied to glass or other nonabsorbent grounds, then swirled, textured, or patterned by found objects and materials before transferring the paint to paper. The negative prints will be entirely different from the positive plates.

The works of Henry Rasmusen are outstanding examples of indirect painting. The following illustrations merely suggest the mysterious beauty and emotional quality of his color combinations, but the forms alone have a great deal to say. Their messages can be interpreted in infinite ways for they suggest many things, yet never allow the senses to be satiated by total revelation.

Fig. 367. "Daybreak," by Henry Rasmusen, is an indirect painting involving several printing techniques. The initial plate was created by soaking strings in oil paints and arranging them on a sheet of glass. Paper was placed over the arrangement and covered by a firm pad. The strings were then pulled out from between the "sandwich," creating rippling striations of color. When the paints were dry, an overlay printing of other materials was superimposed.

Fig. 368. "Thorns for a Crown," a collagraph by Henry Rasmusen. Printed from creased and folded segments of thin plastic bags used by dry cleaners to protect clothes. (Photo courtesy of the artist.)

Fig. 369. "Dante's Inferno," a monotype-collagraph by Henry Rasmusen. Printed from a collage made of crepe-paper scraps, cellophane, wrapping twine, and silk thread. (Photo courtesy of the artist.)

RUBBINGS

For centuries, relief patterns and incised designs on tombstones, monuments, brass tablets, and sculpture have been reproduced by making rubbings of them. The basic technique is known to every child who has placed a sheet of tablet paper over a coin and rubbed it with a pencil to create a negative picture. This is but one approach, however. Rubbings can also be made with inks, colored chalks, crayons, grease pencils, and conté crayons. And in addition to reproducing the patterns of existing works, we can make our own compositions of found materials thereby adding the element of originality to what might otherwise be simply craftsmanship.

Even where the intent is purely to record an interesting surface, the process can involve a great deal more than unimaginative duplication. The quality of the print will be affected by the kind of paper on which it is made, the medium used to produce the image, and above all, the sensitivity of the hands of the "rubber."

To review briefly the most familiar rubbing technique, paper is placed over the surface to be reproduced and taped securely so that it will not slip and create a blurred print. (Plants and other unattached materials should be secured with glue, spray adhesive, or rubber cement to a firm base of cardboard or plywood.) A short length of wax crayon or oil crayon is flattened slightly on one side by rubbing it on a piece of sandpaper. It is then rubbed lightly and evenly in a circular motion over the paper to establish the design. A second harder rubbing is made to bring the print into clear focus. Where the surface has large untextured areas, graduations in value will eliminate the monotony of perfectly flat coloration. (See Figure 370.)

Lithograph pencils make denser and blacker rubbings than ordinary graphite pencils. The process is slower than crayon or charcoal rubbings and is best suited to small prints, but the detail is much sharper. The paper is rubbed with the flat side of the lead, not the point.

On rubbings made by these techniques, incised or depressed areas will be white; raised areas or details will be black. It is possible to make resist rubbings of certain surfaces with white wax crayons or oil crayons. When they are brushed quickly with dark water color, the ink rolls off the wax and adheres only to the background, leaving a delicate white image of the elevated pattern.

There are several drawbacks to this technique, however. It is somewhat laborious, and is most successful on hard surfaces having strong relief designs. Most fresh plants are too soft to withstand the necessarily vigorous treatment. It is important to use a tough paper since extra pressure is required to make the deposit of wax quite heavy. The best papers for wax-resist drawings are those designed for watercolor. But since they are fairly thick, they obliterate some of the detail on the underlying surface when they are used for rubbings.

Best results can be obtained with a good quality tissue paper or rice paper, but it is simpler to make white-on-black prints by the process described in Figure 373.

Fig. 370. Pressed ink-stick rubbing on rice paper of an ancient shamanistic stone carving from Malaysia. Shamanism is a type of religion based on the belief that human fate, either good or bad, can be controlled by intercessors or conjurers. Symbolic art played an important role in their magic. (Collection of the author.)

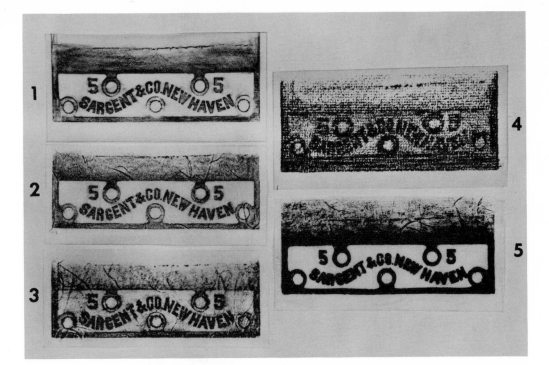

Fig. 371.   RUBBING SAMPLER
1. Tracing paper was taped over an old hinge and a sheet of carbon paper taped face down on top of it. A cover sheet of tracing paper was rubbed firmly with a hard lead pencil to make a carbon copy of the hinge on the first layer of paper. Carbon, pencil, and charcoal rubbings should be sprayed with fixative to prevent smearing.
2. Lithograph pencil rubbing on rice paper.
3. Wax crayon rubbing on rice paper.
4. Charcoal rubbing on charcoal paper.
5. Rice paper was pressed into the pattern of the hinge with a damp sponge and allowed to become almost dry. The relief was then rubbed with a tightly twisted cotton swab barely dampened in waterproof ink.

FISH AND LEAF PRINTS

The exact origin of fish printing is obscure, but Japanese craftsmen are credited with reviving it in the twentieth century. The technique (called Gyotaku) is usually classed as a kind of rubbing, but it is probably closer to printmaking since ink is applied to the fish itself and paper is pressed against it.

The fresh fish is first washed thoroughly, wrapped in paper towels, and blotted until it is as dry as possible. It is then placed on heavy cardboard so that fins and tail can be attractively fanned out and secured with pins. (A few smears of white glue on the cardboard will help hold them in place.) Several coats of charcoal fixative are sprayed on the fish and allowed to dry before removing the pins. Waterproof ink is brushed quickly on the surface, then pounced lightly with a fine sponge dampened in ink to blot up excess pigment which collects around the scales and in depressions.

Water-soluble block printing ink is easier to work with because it does not run and dries more slowly. However, the print will smear if it comes in contact with moisture. The drying time of waterproof ink can be delayed by using a mixture of two drops of glycerine to fifteen drops of ink.

A good grade of rice paper is carefully laid

over the fish and starting at one end, it is "finger-rubbed" lightly until the paper is in contact with the entire surface. A second sheet of paper is then placed over it to absorb ink that may seep through the first layer and be smeared when it is given a final rubbing with a soft cloth or a ball of facial tissue.

A second print made without reinking is usually quite light, but sometimes reveals delicate details which are not evident in the first.

The print is set aside to dry before smoothing out the wrinkles with a warm iron and mounting it on a heavy backing as described for the paper cutouts in Chapter 3. An alternate method for flattening a waterproof print is to place it on a sheet of glass and tamp it down from the middle outward with a damp sponge so that it clings smoothly. The paper will dry flat.

Although this is the usual method for making fish prints, a more detailed pattern can be obtained by a different technique. Using a damp sponge, a sheet of paper is tamped against an *un*-inked fish until it fits like a second skin. When the paper is not quite crisp-dry, it is dry-brushed lightly with a tightly twisted cotton swab dampened in ink. (The swab should be rolled on a paper towel before touching it to the paper or the deposit will be too heavy.) Successive rubbings will build up the color to the desired intensity, as shown in leaf print in No. 3 in Figure 373.

Fig. 372. "Flounder" by Joan Sestak. Waterproof ink print on rice paper. A number of test prints were pulled to work out the proper timing between inking the fish and making the rubbing. Pulled too soon, the print was splotchy. Pulled too late, the image was faint. The artist found best results were obtained when the ink was allowed to dry for two minutes before rubbing the paper against it.

Fig. 373.   LEAF-PRINTING SAMPLER

1. Waterproof ink mixed with glycerine was brushed on a large leaf, covered with a sheet of rice paper and "finger rubbed" lightly. A cover sheet of rice paper (to absorb excess ink) was placed on top of it and rubbed firmly with a soft cloth.

2. Waterproof ink print on watercolor paper.

3. Rice paper was pressed against the leaf with a damp sponge, allowed to dry, then rubbed with a cotton swab dampened with waterproof ink, creating a reverse pattern.

4. White block printing ink was brushed on the leaf and covered with black construction paper. The paper was rubbed with a ball of facial tissue.

5. A second print made without reinking the leaf produces a lighter, more delicate pattern.

FOIL RELIEFS

Relief compositions of materials which are moderately hard and flat can be attached to a firm backing and plated with copper, brass, or aluminum foil. Most professional craftsmen prefer "tooling" metal, which is strong yet flexible enough to reveal in perfect detail the shapes and textures of the underlying materials. However, good results can be obtained with heavy duty household foil as long as the relief does not include sharp protrusions which might perforate the metal, or deep depressions over which the metal would split under pressure of the rubbing implements.

Household foil is actually better for relief patterns of leaves and other delicate materials, since it is thinner, and can be molded more closely against them. Because of its economy and availability, it is especially appropriate for tests and student experiments.

Although procedures for working with the two weights are essentially the same, a few important differences should be noted. Selectivity in the choice of relief materials has already been mentioned. In addition, household foil is not as springy as tooling metal and is inclined to slip out of place as the rubbing proceeds. To eliminate this problem, the surface of the relief and one side of the foil are sprayed with adhesive and joined with coated sides facing. Starting from the center and working outward, the metal is gently hand-pressed to expose the relief pattern and smooth out wrinkles. Excess metal is folded around the edges of the block and taped on the back side.

The metal must now be painstakingly ironed into the relief until it assumes the shape of every detail. (It should not be forced or the foil may tear.) Tooling implements should be firm but somewhat resilient to iron out the metal without damaging it. They can be improvised by sharpening typewriter pencil erasers to points of various sizes, and rounding the tips with sandpaper. Twisted paper tortillons and stumps used to blend pastel and charcoal drawings are also good, as are strips of firm

leather, and special shapes sliced from an old rubber shoe heel.

The finished relief is sprayed flat black and rubbed once more with a smooth cloth wrapped around the finger to clean the paint from the high spots.

Tooling metal will remain in place without glue if it is folded around the block and taped. Since it is heavier than foil, tooling implements must be smooth and rigid. Wooden modeling tools are handy and the ends of brush handles can be sanded into useful shapes. Lengths of wooden dowels can be carved into rounded points and blunt skew chisels.

The metal can either be left on the block as described for household foil, or it can be carefully removed, placed upside down on a level surface, and the margins folded up to make a shallow pan. A thin layer of plaster is poured into the pan and allowed to become firm. A fresh batch of plaster is then added to build up a slab from 1 to 2 inches thick, depending on the size of the relief. (Large panels should be reinforced with screening.)

Surplus metal is folded to the back of the hardened core and the surface is antiqued. Copper reliefs are especially striking when they are darkened with a solution of liver of sulfur or are patinated by one of the other processes outlined in Chapter 4. When patination is completed, the surface can be buffed gently with fine steel wool to reveal some of the original copper color.

ASH PATTERNS IN FUSED GLASS

Glass laminations are generally fused together in the temperature range of 1325–1500° F, according to the hardness or softness of the product. With far less heat than this, plants will disintegrate into fine ashes. Yet surprisingly enough, the characteristic patterns of the ash residue can be preserved with remarkable clarity between the layers of a fused glass slab. The delicate patterns reveal cellular structure which is not clearly evident in the positive forms. Perhaps they seem especially marvelous because we have had a hand in their transformation and, therefore, have a creator's pride in the accomplishment.

These fired images can be framed separately and grouped on a wall, they can be set in a wooden construction for a hanging light, or they can be leaded together into a window, divider, or a segmented panel. The slabs can also be attached to a framed backing covered with felt. Soft medium value colors, such as avocado green, dull gold, medium gray, and medium brown are most effective.

The glass is attached to the felt by thin lines of white glue applied around the edges of the slab. The pieces should be weighted lightly until the adhesive is dry. Wood spacers can be arranged between them as described for clay impressions later in this chapter, or several layers of plastic metal can be squeezed between the crevices of the slabs to build up a raised grid which will strengthen the structure and obscure any visible tracery of glue. When the plastic is sanded to remove sharp peaks and is burnished with the back of an old spoon, the glass appears to be set in a hand-forged metal frame.

But before contemplating the design possibilities of this technique, a comprehensive series of tests should be fired to learn what happens to the plant matter in the firing process, what kinds of images it forms, and how it should be arranged between the layers of glass to make the best pictures. In most cases, the ashes will be white or pale gray. They will look different, however, under colored glass.

Either green or dried plants can be used as long as they are not too bulky, but it is best to remove most of the water from begonias and other succulent plants by pressing them for several days between blotters or paper towels under a weight. It is easier to arrange all materials if they are flattened at least overnight under a stack of magazines.

Watery plants will shrink more than sturdy fibers, but all plants shrink considerably when they are burned. This must be taken into account when they are composed on the base layer of glass or the fired composition will probably be too skimpy. The plants in Figure 375 originally came within ⅛ to ¼ inch of the edges of the glass. The fired results indicate that fuller compositions of superimposed materials would be more interesting. It is simpler to anticipate shrinkage of pressed and dried materials, and it is far easier to align the edges of the glass sandwich that contains them.

Dabs of rubber cement can be used to temporarily secure the arrangement. The sandwich can be held together with short strips of cellophane tape, but it must be attached carefully and rubbed with a soft cloth or fingerprints may remain on the fired piece.

The ash patterns are sharper if the laminations are fired a little lower than the temperature ordinarily used for fused slabs. (Since the glass will be framed in some manner, perfectly rounded edges are not essential.) Here again, tests plus careful records of the results are important. The laminations are fired as described in Chapter 6, giving special attention to raising the temperature slowly until all the dark smoke has burned away. The kiln should be well vented up to this point. The lid can then be closed and firing can proceed more rapidly.

Fig. 374. Pairs of matching blanks are cut from single- or double-strength window glass and flattened plants are secured to the lower blanks with small dabs of rubber cement. Upper blanks are placed on top, with edges carefully aligned. These are test pieces designed to determine how much the plants will shrink and which will make the best designs.

Fig. 375. Several batches of tests fired to different temperatures will reveal the range within which the ash patterns are most successful. The ferns and cedar twigs at the top were fired until the glass had fused together, but edges were not fully rounded. With 50 degrees more heat, the edges of the bottom slabs were rounded and the patterns less perfect, but this is partly due to the delicacy of some of the plants.

Fig. 376. Thin materials that are pressed perfectly flat should have additions of heavier twigs or seeds to elevate the upper blank slightly during the early firing period. Otherwise, gases may be trapped inside the slab, forming large bubbles or dark smoke.

SILHOUETTES ON GLASS

Unfired Plant Patterns

Stencils cut from paper or cardboard can be secured to glass with rubber cement and peeled away after the area around them is painted. Any remaining residue of glue can be rubbed off after the paint is dry. This is impractical for delicate or lacy plant materials, however, since it is almost impossible to apply a thin, all-over coating of rubber cement to hold them flat against the glass so that a clear silhouette is obtained.

If the plants are dried and moderately durable, they can be fastened down with a water-soluble paste and soaked off in cold water after the paint is thoroughly dry. Fresh plants are usually too tender for this method, but they can be coated thinly with a rubbery spray adhesive,[2] then pressed onto the glass and sprayed with flat black paint. Because of the adhesive's flexibility, the plants can be carefully lifted off with a toothpick as soon as the paint has lost its gloss. Spots of adhesive re-

[2] See Index of Supplies.

maining on the glass will be quite visible on the working side, but they are completely unnoticeable when the piece is turned over and set on a white backing or a sheet of metallic tea paper.

The silhouettes are crisper when plants are preflattened as described in the preceding section. If a sharper delineation of stems and outlines is desirable, bits of paint can be carefully scraped away with a toothpick.

This simple idea can be carried further with variations of the techniques for leafing glass in Chapter 6. After making a black silhouette, the design in Figure 377 was misted lightly with brown and green translucent paints. When the paint reached the sticky stage, gold leaf was dropped on top of it. The leaf was pressed lightly against the glass with a soft brush, but no attempt was made to smooth it for several hours. With the air shut off, the paint dries slowly, and the plating can be damaged if it is buffed too soon.

Although nonglare glass costs about twice as much as ordinary window glass, it adds a soft waxy finish to the silhouettes and eliminates blinding reflections on pieces which are hung facing the light.

Fig. 377. PLANT SILHOUETTES ON GLASS
One side of the plants in the foreground was coated lightly with a flexible spray adhesive and pressed against the glass. A thin mist of black paint was sprayed over them and allowed to dry. The large fern frond and other leaves were then attached and the glass was sprayed solid black. When the paint was dry, the plants were peeled away and the glass was gold leafed.

Fired Silhouettes

By substituting ceramic materials for the paints and gold leaf on unfired silhouettes, similar patterns can be made on fused glass. For a single layer of glass, the plant stencils are glued down with tiny dots of rubber cement or spray adhesive and the surrounding area is stippled with black glass color. (A fine textured sponge barely dampened in the color is easy to control.) The stencils are then peeled away, and when the color is dry, the glass is positioned painted side down on a prepared mold or kiln shelf, and fired. Colored glass can be used or the upper surface can be coated with a glass glaze.[3]

Laminated silhouettes have greater depth and are richer against a backing of metallic overglaze. Two matching blanks are cut and cleaned, and the subsurface of the lower blank is coated with gold, platinum, or silver overglaze. (Subtle, muted effects can be obtained

[3] Rubber cement will burn away without marking the glass. Flexible spray adhesives may leave a slight tracery on the surface of a fired sheet, but it is unnoticeable when the silhouette is fired painted side down, or when it is used inside laminations.

with copper luster, but since it is quite dark, the silhouettes will be more shadowy.)

The overglaze is fired until the oils are burned away, as was described for the enameled tiles in Chapter 6.

On the subsurface of the upper blank, the plant stencils are glued down, stippled with black glass color, and allowed to dry. The lower blank is positioned on the shelf or mold *gold* side down. The upper blank is placed on top with *painted* side down. The lamination is then fired until it is fused smoothly together with edges rounded.

The stenciling instructions for the laminated bowl in Figures 378 to 381 are also applicable for unlaminated forms. However, if the material used to create the image has a fairly uniform overall pattern, the design is more interesting when one silhouette is superimposed over another to create illusions of floating shadows.

The most versatile molds for sagging glass have wide rims, which permit the use of blanks which are different in outline from the shape of the cavity. The round mold in Figure 380 has a squarish depression, but the glass blanks are modified teardrops. The cutting pattern was determined by placing a sheet of tracing paper on the mold and marking the boundaries of the rim and well. The teardrop was sketched to fit within this border, leaving a margin of about ½ inch between the edges of the glass and the outside circumference of the mold.

Two identical blanks were cut from double strength window glass.[4] However, as shown in the finished example, they were not arranged on the mold in exact alignment.

A coarse net was soaked in gum solution (used for glazes and copper enamels) and pressed onto the glass with a saturated sponge. While the net was wet, it was pulled and stretched to modify the regularity of the weave. Color was not applied until the gum was completely dry.

Tinted glass blanks can be arranged on the

[4] Instructions for cutting glass are in Chapter 6.

mold with painted sides up. If the upper surface of colorless glass is to be coated with glaze, the painted sides must be down. In this case, the glass must be set carefully on the mold so that the silhouettes are not scratched. Glaze must not be applied to the edges of the glass or it may flow underneath and pick up flakes of the separator.

Fig. 378. Coarse net is secured to two matching glass blanks with glaze gum. When the gum is dry, a sponge saturated with black glass color is pounced lightly over the glass, shading from a heavy application around the outside edges to a paler tint in the center.

Fig. 379. When the paint is dry, the net is peeled away.

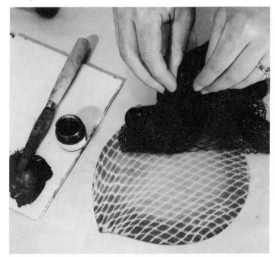

Fig. 380. The lower blank is centered over the cavity, painted side down, with its tip following the line of one corner of the squarish cavity. The upper blank is placed on top, painted side down, with its tip pointing in the opposite direction. Colored glass glaze is sponged on the exposed surface, taking care to leave the cut edges clean.

Fig. 381. The glass is fired until it has sagged into the mold and edges are rounded.

IMPRESSIONS IN CLAY

The first impressions in clay were made millions of years ago, long before man existed on this planet. Under certain conditions, many imprints of plants, insects, and animal tracks gradually hardened into rocks and have survived to the present time.

Beginning craftsmen immediately respond to the complete submissiveness of clay. It can be rolled into a ball, poked with a finger, and a hole will remain to record the exact size and shape of the finger. After observing this, they quickly graduate to making large pancakes that will retain the imprint of an entire hand. It seems magical that the hand is so faithfully reproduced, yet its image is different from its reality. It is even more interesting, perhaps, since it is less familiar. The wonder increases with the discovery that all other objects also have negative images, and when seen in reverse, details which were previously overlooked come into focus and appear to be new.

A damp string dropped at random on a clay slab and patted or rolled into the surface will leave a meandering incised trail which has a character that cannot be deliberately produced by tools. The textures of broken bits of styrofoam, dry sponges, shells, coral, chains, bark, feathers, and countless other trivial components of our environments are equally fascinating to study, and they lead to exciting discoveries.

Clay is not submissive indefinitely, of course. Exposure to air and warmth of the hands causes it to gradually become dry and crumbly. Students should be given only small quantities at a time and be taught how to preserve its plasticity with damp rags.

Impressions of the kind demonstrated in the following projects are simple enough to be adapted to the capabilities of almost any school age group, yet they are challenging enough to interest an adult. The clay should be put in good modeling condition by wedging and pounding it thoroughly to eliminate air bubbles. It should be soft and malleable, but not sticky enough to cling to the fingers. The addition of 10 to 20 percent fine grog will decrease shrinkage and lessen the chance of warpage.

If a number of impressions are designed for assembly into a large panel, decorative materials (leaves, flowers, keys, and the like) should be arranged on scored paper to determine the proportions of the separate tiles. Since it is difficult to estimate in advance exactly how much the clay will shrink, it is best to cut the backing after the pieces are fired.

Clay impressions can be finished by most of the classic techniques for finishing pottery. Aside from the method described here, they can be glazed, they can be bisqued and rubbed with unfired ceramic stains, or they can be painted with earthy underglaze colors, sponged to remove pigment from the high spots, then coated with a clear matte glaze.

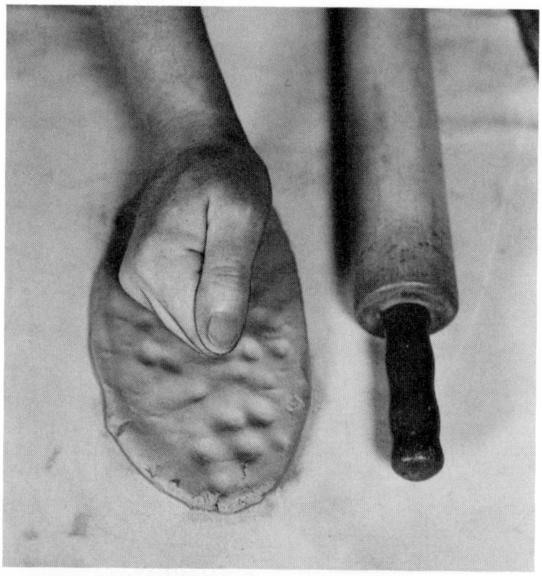

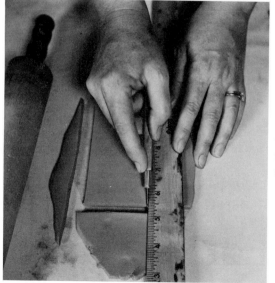

IMPRESSIONS IN CLAY

Fig. 382. Grogged modeling clay is wedged to remove air pockets, then pounded into a large pancake on the cloth side of a sheet of oilcloth.

Fig. 383. The clay is rolled into an even slab between strips of wood ¼ to ⅜ inch thick, and trimmed to size.

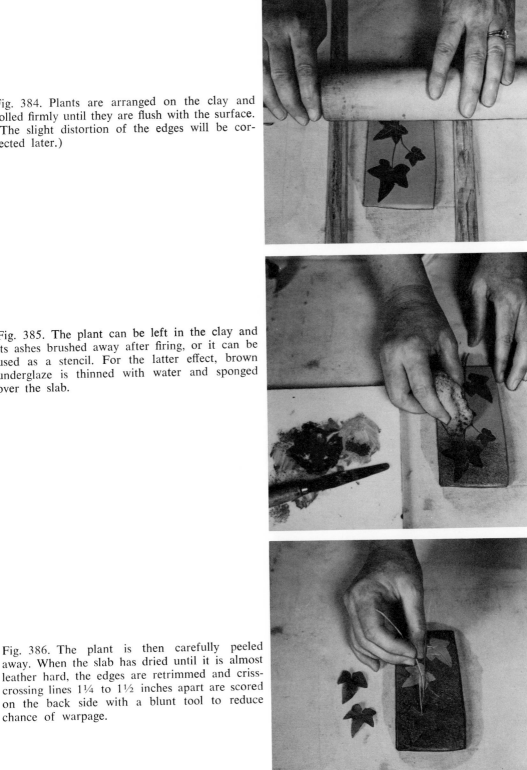

Fig. 384. Plants are arranged on the clay and rolled firmly until they are flush with the surface. (The slight distortion of the edges will be corrected later.)

Fig. 385. The plant can be left in the clay and its ashes brushed away after firing, or it can be used as a stencil. For the latter effect, brown underglaze is thinned with water and sponged over the slab.

Fig. 386. The plant is then carefully peeled away. When the slab has dried until it is almost leather hard, the edges are retrimmed and crisscrossing lines 1¼ to 1½ inches apart are scored on the back side with a blunt tool to reduce chance of warpage.

Fig. 388. When all the tiles are finished, they are arranged with wood spacers on paper to determine the size of the backing. The backing is framed, buttered with tile mastic, and the impressions and spacers are pressed in place one at a time.

Fig. 387. The tile is dried between paper towels under a light weight, and the sides are rubbed on fine sandpaper to remove any protrusions. After firing, it is brushed with a brown antiquing stain and the high spots are wiped clean.

Fig. 389. This arrangement is a study in cool and warm browns. Some of the plants were used as stencils; others are impressions alone. Split redwood strips separate the tiles. The entire panel was coated with a penetrating waterproofing sealer before hanging it on an exterior deck.

IMPRESSIONS IN MODELING PLASTIC

A plastic modeling compound which can be cured in the kitchen oven makes an admirable substitute for clay in certain kinds of projects. It does not have the same feel of clay, and is not as versatile. On the other hand, it does not dry out from exposure to air, which is one of the problems associated with clay projects in the classroom and in limited home workshops. It also does not shrink during the curing process, which means that unlike clay, it will not crack around embedments of pebbles, bits of glass, coins, metals, and other nonflammable materials.

When it is first removed from its package, the plastic is quite firm and somewhat inflexible. After it is squeezed and kneaded in the hands a few minutes, it becomes soft and pliable. It is more resilient and rubbery than clay, and is not as readily rolled into an even sheet. It is helpful to stretch and pat a handful into a large pancake before flattening it with a rolling pin.

Large sheets are difficult to handle and pieces thicker than 1 to 1½ inches are inclined to develop surface fissures when they are heat cured. It is wise to make large panels in sections and assemble them on a backing after they are hardened and colored. White glue or epoxy can be used as an adhesive, and the joints can be filled with tinted wood putty, or grout, or separated by strips of wood as shown in Figure 389.

The cured plastic retains a certain resiliency and does not have the hard, brittle qualities of fired clay. This suggests both advantages and disadvantages which should be considered when evaluating its suitability for a particular project.

To cure the finished forms, they are arranged on a foil-lined cookie sheet and placed in a cold oven. They are heated 15 minutes at 200 degrees, 15 minutes at 250 degrees, 15 minutes at 300 degrees, then removed immediately. A small amount of smoke will be created, and the color may be slightly darkened. If the pieces are brown, however, they have been overcooked. Too much heat can also cause cracks.[5]

Dyes, acrylic paints, and acrylic mediums can be used to replace ceramic colorants and glazes. Lacquers and paints containing turpentine are not recommended because they have a tendency to make the surface slightly sticky.

Fabric dyes are useful for quickly coloring beads and small objects. A fairly concentrated solution is mixed first and brought to a boil. The container is removed from heat, and a few test balls are dropped in and stirred for several minutes. After rinsing the balls they should be allowed to dry before making any adjustments in the intensity of the color.

Dyed beads can be sealed with transparent acrylic medium or liquid wax. By inserting toothpicks through the holes they can be impaled on a block of styrofoam to dry. The impressions are more dramatic if they are antiqued after the medium is hard. This can be done by brushing them with dark acrylic colors and buffing the high spots clean.

[5] These curing instructions were arrived at after many experiments. They vary somewhat from those suggested by the manufacturer.

IMPRINTED PLASTIC BEADS

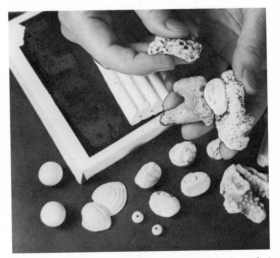

Fig. 390. Plastic modeling compound is kneaded until it is soft and pliable, then rolled into balls of graduated sizes. The balls are pressed against bits of coral, seeds, and shells. A number of small pellets are made to use as spacers, as well as an elongated form for a pendant.

Fig. 391. Holding the beads gently so that the impressions are not blurred, they are perforated with a round toothpick or large needle. The opening is refined by twirling the toothpick lightly through each end of the hole. The beads are heat cured, then tinted with olive green and brown fabric dyes.

Fig. 392. The dyed beads are suspended on toothpicks, coated with clear matte acrylic medium and arranged on a block of styrofoam to dry. They are then antiqued with darker acrylic colors and strung on heavy linen thread, thin strips of leather, or fishing line.

Fig. 393. Paperweights with "mirror messages" can be made by cutting out words and letters from newspapers and rolling a patty of modeling plastic over them. The reversed print can be read in a mirror.

Fig. 394. The ceramic paperweight at the bottom was made by the method described for the tiles in Figures 382 to 389. This shows the negative image of the leaf. Similar impressions can be used as molds to make positive designs with modeling plastic, such as the coaster at the top. The circle was cut out with the rim of a can. The cured coaster was dyed and antiqued as described for the imprinted beads.

POTTERY FROM IMPRESSIONS

Natural forms have inspired pottery designs since man first learned how to shape and harden clay, and it is not our intention to actually duplicate them, but rather to use their shapes as starting points from which to develop new forms.

Impressions from gourds, melons, squash, and other firm vegetables make interesting cores for building ceramic forms. The object is oiled and a line is marked around it to divide it into halves, either vertically or horizontally. (A few toothpicks inserted on the line will keep it from becoming obscured under the clay coating.) Several layers of paper towels are tamped against the form with a damp sponge. When the paper is partly dry, a sheet of clay about ½ inch thick is draped over the core, pressed firmly against it, and trimmed just beneath the protruding toothpicks.

The clay must be removed from the core as soon as it is firm enough to handle or it will crack. The rim is then refined and the inside can be smoothed or textured. The outside can be modeled in any fashion which is in character with the shape.

Molds from Natural Forms

The usual methods for making plaster molds are described in many good books on ceramics, but the entirely different approach presented here greatly simplifies making impressions of objects which have slight undercuts.

An undercut is an inward curve or angle on a shape which would create a lock within a rigid encasement. For example, only half of the squash in Figure 396 can be molded in one piece and the division must be made at its equator. If the casing were extended to a point where the form began to decrease in circumference, the squash could not be pulled out. The small nodules on the gourds in Figure 395 would also create undercuts.

Forms with undercuts are ordinarily molded by either eliminating minor protrusions, or making the mold in several pieces. Flexible rubber or plastic molds which can be peeled away from the hardened core are practical for plaster or plastic castings. Ceramic molds, however, must be rigid and absorbent enough to draw water from the clay.

The process shown in Figures 395 to 402 offers a unique solution. It begins with a shell of surgical plaster bandage which needs only to be dipped in water to be ready for use.[6]

Several layers will create a fairly durable shell which will harden in less than thirty minutes. The shell has sufficient flexibility so that it can be freed from shallow undercuts by lifting the edges slightly and twisting it gently until the suction is broken. With a few pats, it can be returned to its original shape.

Either the outside or inside surface of this basic form can be used for a clay casting. The *convex* side creates the mold in the illustrated project. To use the inner *concave* surface, the mold would be prepared in a cardboard box at least 1¼ inches larger in all directions than the shell itself. Seams of the box must be well taped, and the inside oiled. A layer of plaster is poured in the box and allowed to set until it will support the shell in an upright position. When this layer is firm, fresh plaster is mixed and poured around the shell until it is level with the top edges.[7]

At this point, the mold should be examined to determine whether or not minor undercuts will create a problem when it is cast. If they are not deep, the shrinkage of the clay will usually free the form. However, deep undercuts should be corrected with plaster. Once these additions are hard, the cavity of the mold can be smoothed and made more absorbent by pouring in a small amount of plaster, swirling it around until the entire surface is coated, then pouring out the excess.

[6] This material is used for casts on broken limbs and may be obtained from pharmacists. Similar material is also available in kits. See Index of Supplies.

[7] Dry plaster forms should always be thoroughly dampened before adding fresh layers to them. Cement additives may be purchased to improve the bonding qualities of both plaster and mortar.

Molds made by these methods are not designed to produce rigidly perfect forms, like commercial greenware, which are refined by merely removing a few seam lines or irregularities. They should be regarded as convenient impressions which can be cast, then remodeled into original objects.

MAKING A POTTERY BOWL FROM A PLASTER IMPRESSION

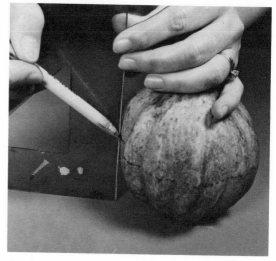

Fig. 396. A large squash is an ideal subject. It is first set upright on a pellet of floral clay, and its equator is marked with waterproof ink. A ruler or triangle should be used to make the mark an equal height from the table all the way around.

Fig. 395. Impressions of forms with simple contours can be made with surgical plaster bandage and used as cores or shells for ceramic molds. Shallow undercuts will not create problems, but nodules, such as those on the right-hand gourd, should be carved off.

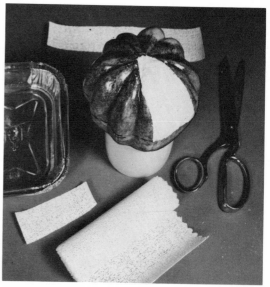

Fig. 397. The squash is oiled lightly with glycerin and blotted with tissue. Surgical plaster bandage is cut into wedge-shaped strips, dipped in water, and smoothed over it. Subsequent additions are overlapped and rubbed to make the surface as smooth as possible. Several layers are built up and allowed to harden.

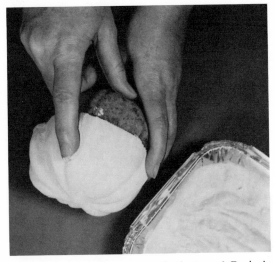

Fig. 398. A small amount of plaster of Paris is mixed with water to a thick consistency and spread over the shell. Extra plaster is added to fill in deep depressions or cups which would create undercuts.

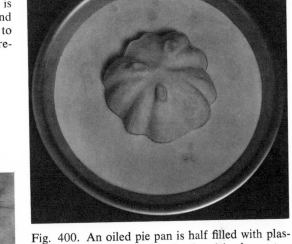

Fig. 400. An oiled pie pan is half filled with plaster, and the hardened core is placed in the center. (If the mold is to be left in disposable pans, the oil is unnecessary.) To use the impression for making a mold for sagging glass, three feet are added so that the bowl will not rock. (The resulting depressions in a ceramic casting are filled with pellets of clay.) The plaster mold is refined by pouring a final thin layer of plaster over the entire surface.

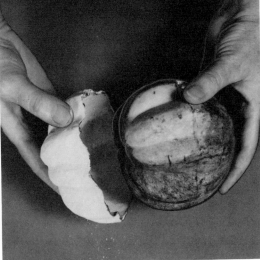

Fig. 399. When it has set, the shell is gently worked away from the core. To use the outside surface for casting, it is set upright on a patty of floral clay and filled with plaster.

Fig. 401. When the mold is dry, overlapping pellets of terra-cotta clay are pressed firmly against it to build up a rind about ½ inch thick. After shaping it roughly with a modeling tool, the thickness is checked by inserting a marked toothpick into the rind in a number of places. Clay is then added or scraped away to make the walls as uniform as possible. This example was imprinted with a piece of coral.

Fig. 402. To release the clay from the core, the mold is held in one hand and the plaster margin is tapped sharply with the edge of the other hand all the way around the form. The bowl is covered and dried upside down before smoothing the rim and the bottom on fine sandpaper, and cleaning away the dust with a damp sponge. An interesting contrast is obtained when the inside is glazed and the outside is stained.

To make a mold for sagging glass from the impression in Figure 400, we must first make sure that it stands level, since the impression will form the *outside* of the glass bowl instead of the *inside* of a clay bowl. Three pellets of bandage can be smoothed on the bottom to serve as feet to keep the glass from rocking. The sides of the feet must be sloping so that no undercuts are created. When they are firm, the plaster form is set on a level table so that the height from the table top to plaster base can be measured all around. The feet are then sanded to make any necessary adjustments.

Clay containing from 15 to 30 percent fine grog is rolled between boards into a sheet from ½ to ¾ inch thick, draped over the plaster core and flat margin around it, and pressed down firmly against them. After trimming away any excess clay which extends beyond the edges of the plaster margin, the clay is left to dry until it can be separated from the mold. The rim is then retrimmed, leaving a margin about 2 inches wide around the cavity. Several small holes are made in the bottom of the mold with a toothpick to prevent air pockets from being trapped under the sagging glass.

When the mold is firm enough to handle, it is refined with a damp sponge and the bottom is sanded so that it stands perfectly level. It is then turned upside down on newspapers or a plaster bat and covered lightly so that it will dry slowly. The mold is fired about two cones lower than the maturity of the clay.[8]

Simple shapes, such as the gourds in Figure 395, can be completely covered with plaster bandage and the hardened shell separated from the core by slicing it into halves with a sharp knife. Each half can be made into a mold and cast with clay as described for the bowl. When the edges are serrated and painted with thick slip, they can be pressed together with a firm, twisting motion. The incision is eradicated by working across it with a smooth modeling tool, adding small pinches of clay where necessary to fill depressions. With an opening cut in the top, the form can be used as the basic shape for a vase or weed pot. It can be redesigned with a foot or neck and carved, textured, or glazed.

Unfired containers can be devised from the shells themselves. The form is covered with several layers of bandage and cut apart as just described. The halves are rejoined by covering the seams with strips of bandage. After reinforcing the shell with another layer or two, an opening is cut in the top. It can then be coated with papier-mâché and finished by one of the techniques noted in Chapter 3. Filled with sand or gravel, it can be used as a vase for dried grasses or flowers made from magazine papers.

IMPRESSIONS IN PLASTER

Plants and other patterned materials can be impressed in either the top or the subsurface of a plaster slab. Sturdy cardboard boxes or disposable pie tins are suitable molds for test

[8] Instructions for sagging glass are outlined in *Mosaic Techniques* by Mary Lou Stribling (New York: Crown Publishers, Inc., 1966).

pieces; large slabs can be poured in an open frame made from boards 3 to 4 inches wide. The wood should be sealed with varnish or shellac, then oiled to keep the plaster from sticking. A sheet of plastic film or aluminum foil is spread on a level table as a backing, and the frame is set in the middle of it. Cracks between the bottom of the frame and the working surface are caulked on the outside with floral clay.

Sand-casting is one of the simplest methods for making impressions and the basic process was described in the previous chapter. Imprints are reversed in the plaster casting. That is, depressed areas and lines will be raised on the finished slab. A layer of clay about ½ inch thick in the bottom of the frame can be similarly imprinted. Clay is more plastic than sand and will faithfully record the most delicate pattern.

To make negative patterns in plaster of flatened plants and rigid objects without undercuts, the area enclosed by the frame is liberally coated with white glue, spray adhesive, or a sticky water-soluble paste, and the decorative materials are pressed into it. When the glue is completely dry, the arrangement is brushed with oil and plaster is poured over it. After the slab is hard, it is removed from the frame and the embedded materials are carefully picked out.

Thin ledges of plaster will almost inevitably run under the embedments in places, but they are easily scraped off. The impressed design can be refined with a sharp knife, and if desired, the composition can be altered by additional incised lines.

Impressions on the surface of plaster slabs are usually combinations of casting and carving, and since the process is more direct, it is easier to control the design. Sydney Herschleb pours slabs on framed hardboard backings and presses textured objects into the plaster just before the mixture sets. After the objects are removed, their imprints are refined with wood carving tools and an assortment of salvaged dental tools.

Fig. 403. "Wild Flowers" by Sydney Herschleb. Ferns, grasses, leaves, flowers, and other objects were pressed in a plaster slab before it had set. Incised lines and carved refinements were added after the plaster was firm. When the slab was completely dry, it was sealed with a thin coat of diluted shellac and strained with washes of oil paints in grayed, stonelike colors. To integrate the work, it was buffed gently with very fine sandpaper.

Appendix

Temperature Equivalents of Cones

Slow firing allows heat to soak through ceramic materials, maturing them (as well as cones) a little sooner than a rapid fire. With a heat rise of less than 300° F. per hour, cones may bend from 25° to 50° F. earlier than the temperatures indicated by the standard cone chart of the Edward Orton Jr. Ceramic Foundation.

Cone 022—1121° F.	Cone 05—1904° F.
Cone 021—1139° F.	Cone 04—1940° F.
Cone 020—1202° F.	Cone 03—2039° F.
Cone 019—1220° F.	Cone 02—2057° F.
Cone 018—1328° F.	Cone 01—2093° F.
Cone 017—1418° F.	Cone 1—2120° F.
Cone 016—1463° F.	Cone 2—2129° F.
Cone 015—1481° F.	Cone 3—2138° F.
Cone 014—1526° F.	Cone 4—2174° F.
Cone 013—1580° F.	Cone 5—2201° F.
Cone 012—1607° F.	Cone 6—2246° F.
Cone 011—1643° F.	Cone 7—2282° F.
Cone 010—1661° F.	Cone 8—2300° F.
Cone 09—1706° F.	Cone 9—2345° F.
Cone 08—1742° F.	Cone 10—2381° F.
Cone 07—1814° F.	Cone 11—2417° F.
Cone 06—1859° F.	Cone 12—2435° F.

Index of Supplies

Materials for working with clay, glass, and copper enameling can be obtained from ceramic supply houses. Most of the other supplies mentioned in the text are available in hardware stores, stationers, and shops carrying art and craft materials. Brand names and manufacturers of special materials are listed here for the convenience of the reader. These are products which were used by the author, and are not intended to imply a lack of merit in similar products which are not included.

Acrylic Paints, Mediums, and Gels

Hyplar
M. Grumbacher, Inc.
460 W. 34th St.
New York, N. Y.

Liquitex Acrylic Polymer
Permanent Pigments, Inc.
2700 Highland Ave.
Cincinnati, Ohio

Adhesives

Concrete Adhesive
Wilhold Glues, Inc.
Santa Fe Springs, Calif., 90670
Chicago, Ill., 60612

Epoxies

E-Pox-e
The Woodhill Chemical Co.
Cleveland, Ohio

Wilhold *Clear Epoxy Glue*
Wilhold Glues, Inc.
Santa Fe Springs, Calif., 90670
Chicago, Ill., 60612

Fabric Adhesive

Glu-Gal
Wilhold Glues, Inc.
Santa Fe Springs, Calif., 90670
Chicago, Ill., 60612

Mastics

Glu-On
Wilhold Glues, Inc.
Santa Fe Springs, Calif., 90670
Chicago, Ill., 60612

Miracle Mastic
Miracle Adhesives Corp.
Bellmore, Long Island,
New York

Tec
Technical Adhesives, Inc.
7415 N. St. Louis Ave.
Skokie, Ill.
San Francisco, Calif.

Paper Paste

Yes
Gane Brothers and Lane, Inc.
Chicago, Dallas, St. Louis, New York,
Boston, Los Angeles, Seattle, San
Francisco

Plastic Adhesives

Dupont Plastic Cement
E. I. du Pont de Nemours and Co., Inc.
Wilmington, Del.

Grapestik (for polyester castings)
Bond Adhesives Co.
Jersey City, N.J., 07303

Plastic Model Cement
Wilhold Glues, Inc.
Santa Fe Springs, Calif., 90670
Chicago, Ill., 60612

Rubber Cements

Carter's Rubber Cement
Cambridge, Mass.

White Rubber Cement
M. Grumbacher, Inc.
460 W. 34th St.
New York, N. Y.

Spray Adhesive

Spray Ment Adhesive
Minnesota Mining and Mfg. Co.
3 M Center
St. Paul, Minn., 55101

White Glues (multi-purpose)

Elmer's Glue
The Borden Chemical Co.
New York, N. Y., 10017

Glu-Bird, and *Craft Heavy Body Glue*
Willhold Glues, Inc.
Santa Fe Springs, Calif., 90670
Chicago, Ill., 60612

Wood Glues

Elmer's Contact Cement
Borden Chemical Co.
New York, N. Y., 10017

Weldwood
U. S. Plywood Co.

ANTIQUING STAINS (wood)

Flecto Antique
The Flecto Co., Inc.
Oakland, Calif.

Tone 'N Tique
C. H. Tripp Finishing Co.
La Jolla, Calif.

(for gold leaf)

Old World Art Antiquing Glaze
and Adhesive
The Conklin-Fenstermaker Co.
5108 N. Calmview Ave.
Baldwin Park, Calif., 91706

BLOCK PRINTING INK

Speedball Water Soluble Ink
(*for block printing*)
Hunt Mfg. Co.
Statesville, N. C.

CAN OPENERS

Ekco
Ekco Housewares Co.
Franklin Park, Ill., 60131

Swing-A-Way
Swing-A-Way Mfg. Co.
4100 Beck Ave.
St. Louis, Mo., 63116

CARVING TOOLS

(wood)

Marples Carving Tools
Wm. Marples and Sons, Ltd.
Sheffield, Eng.

(lightweight materials)

X-Acto
X-Acto, Inc.
L. I. C. 1
New York

CHEMICALS (for patinating metals)

J. T. Baker Chemical Co.
Phillipsburg, N. J.

Van Waters and Rogers, Inc.
San Francisco, Calif.

CLAY (prepared terra-cotta)

Quarry Tile Mix
Navajo Ceramic Clays
Industrial Mineral and Chemical Co.
Berkeley, Calif.

CRAYONS

Binney and Smith, Inc.
380 Madison Ave.
New York, N. Y.

Permanent Pigments, Inc.
2700 Highland Ave.
Cincinnati, Ohio, 45212

DRILLS (electric)

(hobby weight)

Moto-Tool
Dremel Mfg. C.o
Racine, Wis.

(standard)

Black and Decker
Black and Decker Mfg. Co.
Towson, Md.

Stanley
The Stanley Works
New Britain, Conn.

DYES (fabrics)

(for block printing and cold batik)

Versatex
Durable Arts
Box 2413
San Rafael, Calif., 94901

(for dipping)

Rit
Best Foods Division
Corn Products Co.
Indianapolis, Ind.

Tintex
Tintex Corp.
Jamaica, N. Y.

(for stenciling and painting)

Prang Textile Colors
The American Crayon Co.
Sandusky, Ohio

FIXATIVES

(for drawings and rubbings)

Spray Fix
Blair Art Products, Inc.
Memphis, Tennessee

Workable Fixatif
Krylon, Inc.
Norristown, Pa.

FLORAL CLAY

Vogue Floral Clay
Beagle Mfg. Co., Inc.
Pasadena, Calif.

GESSO

Hyplar Gesso and *Hyplar Modeling Paste*
M. Grumbacher, Inc.
460 W. 34th St.
New York, N. Y.

Liquitex Gesso and *Liquitex Modeling Paste*
Permanent Pigments, Inc.
2700 Highland Ave.
Cincinnati, Ohio

GESSO EXTRUDER

Dam-It Gun
Taylor and Art Plastics
Oakland, Calif.

GLASS (ribbed)

(BELGIAN)
Listed as *"Glaverbel,"* by some distributors.
Listed as *"Narrow, fluted, textured pattern #55"* by Northern Calif. Glass Co.

(DOMESTIC)
Pluralite
Mississippi Glass Co.
St. Louis, Mo. (and other cities)

GLASS CUTTERS

(straight cutters)

Fletcher Terry
Bristol, Conn.

(straight and circle cutters)

Red Devil
Red Devil, Inc.
Union, N. J.

GLASS SUPPLIES

(for kiln-fused glass)

Kay Kinney Contoured Glass
725 Laguna Canyon Rd.
Laguna Beach, Calif., 92651
(Glazes: *Glasstain;* separator: *Mold Coat;*
black glass color: *Black Line.*

(unfired colors)
Glass Stain
Stain Glass Products
Cleveland, Ohio

GOLD LEAF AND SIMULATED GOLD LEAF

Old World Art
The Conklin-Fenstermaker Co.
5108 N. Calmview Ave.
Baldwin Park, Calif., 91706

GRAVEL (graded sizes, colored)

Wonder Rock
The Kordon Corp.
Hayward, Calif.

GROUT BINDER

Groutite
Wilhold Glues, Inc.
Santa Fe Springs, Calif., 90670
Chicago, Ill., 60612

GUN BLUE

Brownell's Gun Blue
Birchwood Casey Co.
Minneapolis, Minn.

IMPACT CENTER PUNCH

The L. S. Starrett Co.
Athol, Mass.

LEAD CAME

Bunker Hill
2700 16th Ave. S. W.
Seattle, Wash., 98134

LEAD TAPE (self-adhering)

Scotch Brand Pressure-Sensitive Tapes
Minnesota Mining and Mfg. Co.
St. Paul, Minn.

LOOM (hobby)

Noris Educational Weaving Frame
Made in West Germany, available in the U.S.
  in toy shops, hobby shops, and import
  outlets.

NEEDLES (specialized)

The Singer Company
30 Rockefeller Plaza
New York, N. Y., 10020

PAPIER-MÂCHÉ (prepared pulp)

Celluclay
The Celluclay Co., Inc.
Marshall, Texas

Quick Set Papier-Mâché Mix
Art Brite Chem. Corp.
Jersey City, N. J., 07306

PLASTER BANDAGE (surgical)

Johnson and Johnson
New Brunswick, N. J.

PLASTER CLOTH (kit)

Pariscraft
Pariscraft Co.
P. O. Box 31
New Brunswick, N. J,. 08903

PLASTIC LAMINATING FILM (for fabrics)

Wonder-Under
Pellon Corp.
1120 Ave. of the Americas
New York, N. Y., 10036

PLASTIC METALS

Antique Scroll Leaded Art
Wilhold Glues, Inc.
Santa Fe Springs, Calif., 90670
Chicago, Ill., 60612

Dam-It Simulated Lead
Taylor and Art Plastics
Oakland, Calif.

Duro Liquid Steel
and *Duro Plastic Aluminum*
The Woodhill Chemical Co.
Cleveland, Ohio

PLASTIC MODELING COMPOUND

Sculpey
Polyform Products, Inc.
Schiller Park, Ill., 60176

PLASTIC SHEETS

(decorative, self-adhering)

Con-Tact
Cohn-Hall-Marx
1407 Broadway
New York, N. Y., 10018

POPCORN (colored)

Col-R-Corn
3-Min. Brand

PUTTY (for wood)

Durham's Rock-Hard Water Putty
Donald Durham Co.
Des Moines, Iowa

SEALERS

(flexible marine sealers)

Silastic Clear Sealer
Dow Corning Corp.
Midland, Mich.

Translucent Silicone Rubber Clear Seal
General Electric
Silicone Products Dept.
Waterford, N. J.

(waterproofing sealers)

Brightstone
Bailey's Wax Products
644 Hearst Ave.
Berkeley, Calif.

Tec Silicone Sealer
Technical Adhesives, Inc.
7415 N. St. Louis Ave.
Skokie, Ill.
San Francisco, Calif.

SOIL-RESISTANT SPRAYS (for fabrics)

All-Dri
Schrader Chemical Co., Inc.
Antioch, Calif.

Scotch-Gard
Chemical Division
3-M Co.
St. Paul, Minn.

SOLDER

(air-hardened)

Duratite Liquid Solder
Duratite Div. of DAP
General Offices
Dayton, Ohio

Liquid Solder
Le Pages Liquid Solder
Pittsburgh, Pa.

(heat-fused)

Kester Solder Co.
Div. of Litton Industries
Chicago, Ill., Newark, N. J.

SOLDERING GUN

Weller Soldering Gun
Weller Electric Corp.
Easton, Pa., 18042

SPRAY PAINTS

(all-purpose matte coating)

Blair Spray Matte
Blair Art Products, Inc.
Memphis, Tenn.

(clear finishes)

Krylon
Norristown, Pa.

(transparent, translucent, and
opaque colors)

Soft Spray 'Namel
Pactra Chemical Co.
6725 Sunset Blvd.
Los Angeles, Calif.

TAPE (self-adhering, colored, from 1/64 to 2 inches wide)

Alvin *Graph A Plan*
Windsor, Conn.

TINKERTOYS

A. G. Spaulding and Bros., Inc.
807 Greenwood St.
Evanston, Ill.

TOOLING METALS (aluminum, brass, copper)

Maid-O-Metal

TORCHES AND FUEL (propane)

Bernz O Matic
Bernz O Matic Corp.
Rochester, N. Y.

Sentry
Sentry Hardware Corp.
Cleveland, Ohio, 44113

Turner
Turner Corp.
Sycamore, Ill.

TJANTINGS

Craftools, Inc.
Woodridge, N. J.

TUNGSTEN CARBIDE ROD

TC Rod Saw
Remington Arms Co., Inc.
Bridgeport, Conn.

WAX GILTS

Rub 'N Buff
American Art Clay Co., Inc.
Indianapolis, Ind., 46222

Treasure Gold (also silver, copper, and other
colors)
Connoisseur Studios
Louisville, Ky., 40207

Bibliography and
Suggested References

BOAS, FRANZ. *Primitive Art*. New York: Dover Publications, Inc., 1955.

CASSOU, JEAN. *Georges Braque*. New York: Harry N. Abrams, Inc., 1957.

CHAVATEL, GEORGE. *Exploring with Polymer*. New York: Reinhold Publishing Corp., 1966.

CHENEY, SHELDON. *A World History of Art*. New York: The Viking Press, Inc., 1937.

CHRISTENSEN, ERWIN O. *The Index of American Design*. New York: The Macmillan Co., 1950.

CHRISTENSEN, ERWIN O. *Primitive Art*. New York: Bonanza Books, n.d.

DIVINE, J. A. F., and BLACHFORD, GEORGE. *Stained Glass Craft*. Peoria, Ill.: Manual Arts Press, 1940.

GOLDWATER, ROBERT. *Primitivism in Modern Art* (rev. ed.). New York: Vintage Books, 1967.

HANSEN, H. J. *European Folk Art*. New York and Toronto: McGraw-Hill Book Company, 1968.

HISCOX, GARDNER D. (ed., Eisenson, Harry E., rev. ed. 1956). *Henley's Twentieth Century Book of Formulas, Processes, and Trade Secrets*. New York: Books, Inc., 1968.

HUTTON, HELEN. *The Technique of Collage*. New York: Watson-Guptill Publications; London: B. T. Batsford, Ltd., 1968.

KENNY, JOHN B. *Ceramic Design*. Philadelphia: Chilton Books, 1963.

KINNEY, KAY. *Glass Craft*. Philadelphia: Chilton Books, 1962.

LICHTEN, FRANCES. *The Folk Art of Rural Pennsylvania*. New York: Charles Scribner's Sons, 1963.

MCKEARIN, GEORGE S. and HELEN. *American Glass*. New York: Crown Publishers, Inc., 1941, 1948.

MEILACH, DONA, and SEIDEN, DON. *Direct Metal Sculpture*. New York: Crown Publishers, Inc., 1965.

POIGNANT, ROSLYN. *Oceanic Mythology*. London: Paul Hamlyn Ltd., 1967.

RASMUSEN, HENRY. *Printmaking with Monotype*. Philadelphia and New York: Chilton Books, 1960.

RASMUSEN, HENRY, AND GRANT, ART. *Sculpture from Junk*. New York: Reinhold Publishing Corp., 1967.

ROBB, DAVID M., AND GARRISON, J. J. *Art in the Western World* (4th ed.). New York and Evanston: Harper and Row, Publishers, 1963.

STRIBLING, MARY LOU. *Mosaic Techniques*. New York: Crown Publishers, Inc., 1966.

TOVEY, RICHARD. *The Technique of Weaving*. New York: Reinhold Publishing Corp.; London: B. T. Batsford, Ltd., 1965.

Glossary

Acrylic Paints: Acrylic polymer plastic colors for art work, which may be thinned with water for wash effects, or thickened with gels for heavy impastos. The paints are permanent and waterproof once they are dry.

Alloy: A mixture of metals.

Anneal: To temper or harden by reducing heat gradually.

Appliqué: A type of fabric design in which decorative motifs are attached to a foundation by stitchery or adhesives.

Bark Cloth: See tapa.

Batik: A process for decorating fabrics in which wax is used to create dye-resistant patterns.

Bisque: Fired and unglazed clay.

Blank: (glass): An undecorated glass form.

Braze: A soldering process for metals which melt at high temperatures.

Came: Channeled strips of lead used to bind glass edges and to join separate glass sections together. (Sometimes spelled *calm.*)

China Paints: Low-fire colorants for decorating glazed ceramic ware.

Collage: A design made of assorted flat materials pasted onto a backing.

Color Value: The relationship of a color to lightness or darkness.

Compatible (glass): Glasses which expand and contract at the same ratio during heating and cooling cycles and can, therefore, be successfully fused together.

Craze: Random surface cracks in fired glaze or glass.

Cubism: A twentieth-century movement in art which rejected traditional concepts of naturalism. By reducing images to geometric planes as seen from different viewpoints, the Cubists sought to create a more profound reality than could be revealed by photographic representation.

Cure: The process of hardening plastic materials with heat or chemicals.

Dadaism: A movement which sought to reduce art to the level of absurdity as a protest against pompousness and sentimentality. A cult of meaninglessness and nihilims.

Design: A composition, scheme, or arrangement. A plan for organizing separate materials into a unified pattern.

Earthenware: Objects made of low-fire clay.

240

Epoxy: A thermosetting resin of great strength and flexibility used for adhesives and embedding.

Flux: A liquifying agent which lowers the melting points of metals and glazes.

Folk Art: Art existing among the people of a region or country. Traditonal folk art designs and techniques are handed down from one generation to the next.

Found Art: Art which is made up in part or entirely of natural or salvaged materials.

Fulgurite: A formation which is created when lightning strikes certain kinds of sandy earth and fuses it into a glassy tube.

Gesso: A compound for sizing canvas or broad to prepare it for painting.

Gesso Paste (*Acrylic*): Acrylic polymer latex emulsion containing a filler of marble dust to thicken it to the consistency of putty.

Glass Separator: A material applied to kiln shelves or molds to prevent glass from sticking to them when it is softened by heat.

Glaze (*Ceramic*): A thin skin of glass used to decorate or waterproof clay, or to color the surface of glass.

Glaze (*Paint*): A transparent wash of color applied over a base coat of paint or gold leaf to create antique effects.

Gold Leaf: Delicate metal tissue used for gilding objects and frames.

Greenware: Unfired clay forms.

Grog: Ground bisque which is added to moist clay for texture and to reduce shrinkage.

Gyotaku: A process developed by Japanese craftsmen for making ink prints of fish.

Kiln: An oven for firing ceramic materials.

Kilnwash: China clay and flint which is mixed with water to the consistency of whitewash and applied to the bottom of the kiln and tops of shelves so that glaze drippings can easily be removed.

Laminate: To bond layers of materials into a single unit.

Leaded Glass: Glass segments which are joined together with lead cames.

Luster: An iridescent, low-fire colorant for glass or glazed clay.

Magnesite: Oxychloride cement used as a setting bed for assemblages and mosaic materials.

Mastic: A flexible rubber-based adhesive for mosaic materals and mixed media compositions.

Mixed Media: Designs composed of many different kinds of materials.

Mold: A form for duplicating a shape.

Monopainting: A type of indirect painting in which paints are applied to various surfaces and materials, then transferred by pressure to a final ground. It combines techniques of printmaking with those of traditional direct painting.

Montage: A type of collage in which multiple images are joined together or superimposed to create illusional effects.

Nichrome: Trademark for an alloy which is resistant to deterioration by heat. Used for elements in kilns and household appliances.

Obsidian: Volcanic glass.

Overglazes: Decorative materials which are applied on top of fired glazes and set by firing again to a lower temperature. The category includes china paints and iridescent and metallic lusters.

Oxidation: Surface coloring or deterioration caused by prolonged exposure to oxygen in the air, or by treatment with chemicals which produce the same effect more quickly.

Patchwork: A type of fabric design in which scraps are stitched together to create a decorative pattern.

Patina: A colored film produced by natural aging or chemical treatment.

Primitive Art: Art produced by a culture which has not developed a written language, or which remains essentially unchanged after a written language has been developed.

Primitivism: An attitude which is concerned with emotion, rather than form, and with fundamentals, rather than superficialities. The term is not necessarily associated with works which are crude or unsophisticated.

Pyrometer: An instrument which registers the interior temperature of ceramic kilns.

Pyrometric Cones: Elongated pyramids of minerals formulated to melt at specific temperatures; used for determining the interior temperature of ceramic kilns.

Rock Crystal: Native pure quartz.

Selvage: The vertical nonraveling edge of woven fabric.

Soldering: A process for joining together sections of metal by heat-fusing them to patches (or fillers) of compatible alloys.

Tapa: The Polynesian term for nonwoven fabric produced by softening and pounding plant fibers into flexible sheets.

Thermal Shock: Internal stresses in ceramic materials created by rapid expansion and contraction from abrupt temperature changes. Acute stresses can result in fractures.

Thermoplastic: Applied to substances which may be repeatedly softened by heat, becoming rigid again after cooling.

Thermosetting: Applied to substances which become permanently hard after exposure to heat.

Tinning: The application of a thin coat of solder to metal parts which are to be heat-fused together.

Tjanting: A small pitcher-shaped instrument with a tiny spout and a long handle, designed for trailing wax-resist patterns on fabrics.

Undercut: A shape which angles or curves inward to form a ledge or protrusion which would lock a casting inside a mold.

Underglaze: A colorant which is applied to greenware or bisqued clay and for permanence is covered with a clear glaze.

Warp: The lengthwise threads in woven fabric.

Weaving: A process for making fabric by interlacing lengthwise and crosswise threads.

Wedging (Clay): Pounding and kneading moist clay to remove air bubbles and distribute colorants or grog evenly throughout the mixture.

Weft (or Woof): The crosswise threads in woven fabric.

Index